More Pr

MW00474990

"A book that touches the soul—and a reminder that there is no depth or height that life takes us where God's love can't reach us."

— DIANE TRIBITT, CEO and Founder of D'Lyric Inspired, Leader of the Houston Vitiligo Awareness Movement

"A joyous testimony of how God orchestrates even the smallest details of our lives for his good! Through powerful stories of purpose, uncertainty, fear, and love, we see that God moves mountains in our obedience. *A Children's House* will leave you encouraged and challenged in your faith, with a renewed determination to live daily to bring glory to our great Father."

— COURTNEY WESTLAKE, Author of *A Different Beautiful*

"A light shines brightly at A Children's House, where hope and healing are poured out on all who enter. Dr. Bree has answered a divine calling to be love in action for God's precious children, and those touched by her healing hands and heart will never be the same."

— CLAIRE FRAZIER, Mother of a patient of A Children's House

"Here is an amazing story of how God works through us when we toss out our plans, let Him in, and allow His will to be done. Dr. Bree is living the life God created for her to live, and it is extraordinary."

— STEPHANIE ALANIS BEDFORD, Previous patient and Camp Discovery counselor

"Dr. Bree shows that only when God is in the center of our lives do we truly find success, happiness, and a way to be the good in the world."

— ALLY ROSA-RAMOS, Patient of A Children's House, Camp Discovery counselor

"Alanna's journey to found A Children's House is an inspiring story of faith and a demonstration of how one person can make a real difference in the lives of others."

— CLIFTON M. SMART III, President, Missouri State University

"A Children's House is a warm, very personal account of a determined physician's faith in action."

— J. KEVIN DORSEY, MD, PhD, Dean and Provost Emeritus, Professor in the Department of Medical Education and Department of Internal Medicine, Southern Illinois University School of Medicine

"Here is a glimpse into Dr. Bree's heart, where her passion for the Lord and for children is evident. You will be caught up in her journey and see that each one of us can be used by God."

— ANNE LUCAS, Director, e3 Partners Medical

"A fine example of what it looks like to live your dream loud and clear in real time with real people. Dr. Alanna has definitely laid it all on the line as she welcomes God's story into hers in the unfolding story of A Children's House."

— DON SAWATZKY, Director of Operations, Under the Same Sun

"Dr. Bree is one of the most inspiring people I've met. Her heart for helping others and having the faith to 'step out of the boat' is truly amazing. I will be picking up every penny I see."

> – SHANNON PICKARD, Pastor of Revive Church,
> Author of *The Choice Is Yours*

"A must-read for anyone pursuing their God-given mission. Dr. Bree has illustrated how difficult the journey of faith, discovery and service can be—but also how God will never let you down. I cannot say enough good things about this book."

> – KURT R. PODESZWA, Camp Director, Camp For All,
> Founder of Journey Consulting

"An incredible journey. Dr. Bree demonstrates in her life and her work what it is like when a Christian is guided by the Holy Spirit."

> – BILL BROWN, Houston Astros broadcaster,
> Author of *My Baseball Journey*

"In children, Dr. Bree is alert to a Silent Working of Good in her life and theirs."

> – MARK DAHL, MD, Professor of Dermatology,
> Mayo Clinic College of Medicine, Past President
> of the American Academy of Dermatology

"Take this amazing journey with Dr. Bree and enjoy reading about how Jesus leads, redeems and restores for the good of others. Thank you, Dr. Bree, for writing this adventure down—and most of all for living it!"

> – GREG FINKE, Executive Director, Dwelling 1:14,
> Author of *Joining Jesus on His Mission*

A Children's HOUSE

A Little Story About a God-sized Dream

Alanna F. Bree, M.D.

STELLAR
COMMUNICATIONS
HOUSTON

To God goes all of the glory for He has done great things for me.

I also want to acknowledge my family for all of their love and support in this endeavor:

Doug, my husband, who is my best friend and source of strength and stability in all things;

Sam, my loving and empathetic son who challenges me to refute the status quo; and

Kendyl, my strong and dedicated daughter who inspires me and has encouraged me to share my testimony.

I am so thankful the three of you have been on this journey with me.

Contents

Acknowledgements

I MUST ACKNOWLEDGE GOD above all else in my life. As Romans 11:36 says, "For from Him and through Him and for Him are all things. To Him be the glory forever! Amen."

I am thankful to God for so many others He has placed in my life who have helped me bring A Children's House from a God-sized dream to a reality here on Earth, including:

My husband, Doug, who I have no doubt was made to complete me. You are my balance and my compass. You keep me grounded. You make the good times better and the bad times bearable. I couldn't imagine my life without you.

My children, Sam and Kendyl. You are my heart and soul, and the most precious gifts God has given me. I hope you always know how very much I love you, and I pray my testimony helps you to know Jesus as your Savior and friend.

My parents, Al and Shirley, I thank you for all you sacrificed and for giving me my spiritual foundation. For my sister, Alicia, for being an inspiration and true friend. For my in-laws, Bill and Pat, for raising such a wonderful son and sharing him with me.

My pastor, Michael, who helped me listen to and obey what God was calling me to do.

Our friends, Tom and Norma, who helped put all the pieces in place with their professional expertise, guidance and encouragement. I truly couldn't have done it without you!

Our realtor, John, for helping me purchase the property. Our banker, Mark, for seeing my vision and helping finance it. Our contractors, Ben and Jerid, for sticking it out and not giving up during the long process of permitting and renovations.

Our branding expert, Kimberley, and her husband, Jason, for helping us share what we stand for with our logo, signage, and website, and for generously supporting our nonprofit. Your creativity and hearts to help others are immense.

Our previous and current board members, Abel, Alana, Andrea, Ashley, Ben, Charles, Chad, Christina, Drew, John, Karen, Kathy, Margaret, Robyn, Susan, and Tom, for your friendship and your willingness to serve.

The Children's Fund, for supporting our mission as we were just beginning and believing in the good we could accomplish together.

Acknowledgements

All of my many family and friends who laughed with me, cried with me, and prayed with me during this journey.

My patients and their families who have given me the privilege of doing a job I love so much. It is a tremendous blessing to be able to be a part of your lives.

Finally, my editor, Ella, for giving me a voice so I can bring my testimony to others. You have a wonderful gift, and I feel lucky that you have shared it with me and our readers.

Introduction

"What is the kingdom of God like? What shall I compare it to?
It is like a mustard seed, which a man took and planted
in his garden. It grew and became a tree, and the
birds perched in its branches."

– LUKE 13:18-19

I ALWAYS KNEW I belonged to God, until the day I started to doubt His existence.

I was eight years old, lying in my bedroom with blue and silver butterfly wallpaper and blue carpet. Doubts had been nagging at my mind. *Could God be real? Where did He come from? What if there's another God and we're wrong in our beliefs? How can I know for sure that He exists? How can I know that my God is the right one?*

It was confusing for a child who had been baptized at just a few weeks old, officially ushered into God's family as my parents, godparents, and church family publicly confessed their faith as a community. They told me that I was His from the beginning. He had created me and known me long before I was born. My baptism just sealed me as one of His.

As part of God's family, I had savored my time at church when I was growing up. It was an old church, as quiet and safe as the rest of our small Midwestern town. It had traditional red carpet and dark wood, with stained glass windows lining the sanctuary and large interior lights

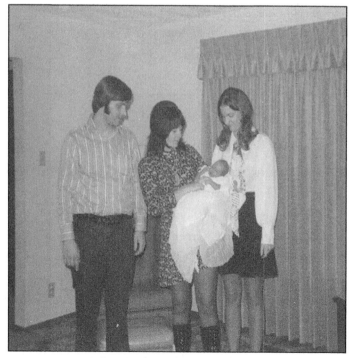

Baptism day with my godparents

hanging on thick chains. A golden cross sat on the center of the altar, which we approached in robes to light candles during service, the floors creaking under us.

Beautiful sounds drifted from that church. The old pipe organ was impressive as it bellowed dramatically, especially during Good Friday services. We sang together, songs that were accompanied by the guitar and piano at Sunday school, and special songs every Christmas Eve at the Christmas pageant. And its smell—its smell was unique. Just a bit musty, yet pleasant, similar to a library. This was periodically admixed with the unforgettable fragrance of slightly damp, warm copies with distinctive blue ink that had just come off the mimeograph machine.

I felt that I belonged there, just as much as I belonged to my two loving, Christian parents. But still the doubts about God's existence tugged at me.

My father had helped to reassure me by reading to me from the Bible and praying with me. But it was his tie tack that he had received from his Sunday school teacher when he was a little boy that gave me an idea. I jumped off my bed and found the tie tack, examining the tiny mustard seed suspended in it. It reminded me of something I'd read in the Bible. In Matthew 17:20, Jesus spoke to His disciples, who were also suffering from unbelief at the time. He said, "Truly I tell you, if you have faith as small as a mustard seed, you can say to this mountain, 'Move from here to there,' and it will move. Nothing will be impossible for you."

I desperately wanted proof that God exists. And if faith "as small as a mustard seed" was truly enough, then that's

My parents, who gave me my spiritual foundation

where I was determined to start. Before I went to bed, I formed a plan. I put a small drop of water the size of a mustard seed in the back corner of my dresser and told God, "If this drop of water is gone in the morning, then I will know that You are real. I will have faith in You and only You."

The next morning, I eagerly checked the back corner of my dresser. The drop of water was gone.

Gone! I couldn't believe it. This was my very own miracle, and it meant everything. It meant that God existed. That was the day that I stopped doubting God—and started believing in Him with a child-like faith.

Introduction

I know what you're probably thinking. There's as good a chance that my mom wiped up the drop of water or that it evaporated as the chance that God came down Himself to take it away. Doesn't seem like much of a miracle, does it? Perhaps not an auspicious start. But whatever happened that day, the drop of water was gone. And my mustard seed of faith had sprouted.

We may not always recognize God at work in us, but when we look back over our lives, we can often see God unfolding the plans He has for us. This is what this little book is all about. I want to tell you about the big plans that God has unfolded in my life since that day in my bedroom—and the mountains He's moved with that mustard seed of faith.

But before I begin, I have a few confessions to make.

- I am a sinful human being. If you know me, then you know I am a very real person with flaws and shortcomings.
- I've had disappointments and failures. You'll read about some of them here.
- I've made many, many mistakes over my lifetime. And unfortunately, I already know I'll make many more.

These admissions would be too difficult to admit if it wasn't for two truths: I am God's creation, and Jesus is my Savior. This means I am made exactly how He wanted me to be, flaws and all. In knowing Jesus, I've realized I am loved beyond measure and forgiven of my sins even though

I don't deserve it. I also know that I no longer need to struggle to find happiness in the world because I have it in Him. I am simply a child of God. This leads to such over-flowing joy that I want to share His love and grace with others so they can experience it too.

This brings me to the reason I'm sharing my story with you. Our stories are not really about us, but more about how God has proven to be faithful in our lives. And so it is with mine. He is a loving and trustworthy God, and I'm so thankful and humbled by the amazing things He has done for me. I pray that my story brings you closer to our great and awesome God and His Son, our Savior, Jesus Christ.

One more thing: I realize that not everyone reading this book is a Christian. Please know that I simply must acknowledge Jesus because He is such a part of my life. I'm hopeful you're not turned away from reading this story; I believe you'll identify with many of my situations. It's not meant to be preachy or overly Christianized, though I do hope it reflects the love of Jesus and helps you to see the amazing things He's doing in our world.

No matter what you or I profess, I firmly believe that we are all children of God and made in His image. I think we all seek Him out in our thoughts and experiences, as we all have a longing to draw closer to Him and seek His life-changing love in our lives. I pray my story will be an encouragement and inspiration to you.

The Angel

---

*"For he will command his angels concerning you
to guard you in all your ways."*

– PSALM 91:11

I WAS NINE YEARS OLD when I met an angel. At least,
that's what I believe was the short, bald man that
showed up at my house, breathless with news. But I'll tell
the story and let you decide.

I was hunched over my desk at school one May afternoon, practicing the slow cursive curves of the alphabet as
my third grade teacher murmured over my shoulder. That
was the year we learned multiplication and watched a
space shuttle launch on TV. Now, as the school year came
to a close, we were all beginning to anticipate the long summer days that were ahead. I gazed out the sunny window as
the minute hand slowly rounded the clock.

Outside, my small Midwestern town was as quiet as my classroom. It was a good, safe place to grow up. A place where you could ride your bike to school or walk to the dime store at the town square with your allowance to buy some little trinket or hang out at the Icee stand with your friends and play video games.

The school bell pierced my thoughts. Finally! I stuffed my handwriting tablet in my desk, grabbed my backpack, and worked my way outside to the bike rack. My friend Rachel and I straddled our bikes and set off, chattering about going to the park to play.

Up ahead, we saw that we were approaching what we called Killer Hill. It was a hill that declined sharply before inclining into a tall, steep grade that put your leg muscles to the test as you tried to ascend it. As always, we peddled as fast as we could down the first slope so that our climb up the incline would be a bit easier.

Down, down . . . I peddled hard down the steep hill, clenching my handlebars tightly as my tire suddenly traversed some loose gravel on the side of the road. My bike wobbled back and forth, more and more erratically, as I tried to stop the bike by frantically pressing on the brakes. But it was to no avail.

That was the last thing I remember.

Later, Rachel would tell me that the next few moments seemed to occur in slow motion. She watched in horror as I flew over my handlebars, skidded a short distance, then landed face-down in the gravel. She ran to me and found me lying in a pool of blood from several injuries to my face and mouth. I was unconscious and unresponsive when she tried to talk to me. Rachel biked quickly back to the school to look for the school nurse.

But when she returned, I was gone.

What transpired next is a matter of conjecture, but the story picks up at my house. My mom had been reading the newspaper when she received a call from a neighbor. He lived near Killer Hill and told her about the accident, repeatedly explaining that I was bloody but that I was going to be okay. He told her there had been a man sitting in his car at the top of the hill when the accident happened who had offered to bring me home. My mom was pacing the hallway when the man pulled into the driveway, and she went running to open the front door.

There stood a short, bald man with the kindest eyes she had ever seen. He seemed a bit anxious as he told her that he had been sitting on the hillside when he had witnessed everything. He breathlessly recounted my fall, saying that he had wanted to stop it from happening, but he just couldn't. He then gently took my mom's hands in his and told her that I was in his car. She blinked in confusion, asking how he knew where to bring me and ready to race out of the house, but he stopped her.

"I want to warn you. She looks bad," he said, giving her hands a light squeeze. "But I know she's going to be fine. You have to believe me that she'll be fine."

My mom peered past him at the car in the driveway. It was a white limousine. I was sitting in the front seat with my face wrapped in a bloodied white towel. She gently

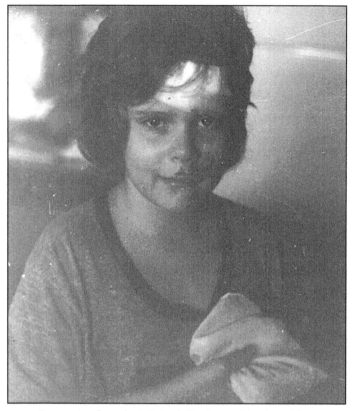

Recovering from the injuries following my bicycle accident

lowered the towel around my head and was taken aback. I was certainly bloody, as she had been warned. She kept repeating to herself in her mind that I would be okay. She could hardly believe there was no blood on the white interior of his car. She noticed a car phone in the console of the front seat, which was quite rare at that time.

With the help of the man, my mom lifted me from the car as I was unable to walk on my own. They carried me into the house with one of them on either side of me. Together, they set me down on a bench just inside our front door. He said he had to go and reassured her again that I would be fine. My mom turned to thank him, but no one was there.

The man was gone.

She quickly glanced down our long cul-de-sac, but there was no sign of the man or his car anywhere to be found. Now, in our town of just over five thousand people, everyone knows everyone else—along with nearly everything about them. Despite asking all around town, no one had seen this man or his white limousine before or after the incident.

There was another detail that left us puzzled. I had been unconscious and in shock when this man picked me up, so I couldn't possibly have given him the route to my house. How did he know where I lived?

That's the day I came to believe that God sends His angels at the right time and to the right place . . . and apparently even equips them with car phones so He can give them directions!

Deferments and Decisions

> *"In their hearts humans plan their course,*
> *but the LORD establishes their steps."*
>
> – PROVERBS 16:9

DEFERRING MEDICAL SCHOOL is one of the best decisions I've ever made. I didn't know it then, but that one year of waiting would change the course of my life.

I had struggled with the decision because it had been a long road getting there—a road that began in 7th grade. Back then, I'd helped tutor children with special needs during my study hall hour. I'd desperately wanted to do something more for those children than just read to them and help them with their activities. The experience inspired me to be a physician. I knew I wanted to dedicate my life to helping children be as healthy as possible.

My desire to be a physician didn't falter in spite of high

school and its typical wild and crazy moments—and more sins than I would like to admit. In spite of the odds, I went on to work hard in college and—amid more sins—study hard for my medical school entrance exam. One night, as I lay in bed in my sorority house, I prayerfully dedicated my life to God's work. I wanted to heal those who were ill if it was His will.

So when I was finally accepted into medical school, I knew I'd received His answer. But because I was initially wait-listed, I made the decision to commit to a research position. Two days after committing to the research position, I received a call from the medical school to let me know they had an unexpected opening and I could start medical school that fall. It was a difficult choice, but I had given my word to my research team, and I deferred my acceptance to medical school for one year.

As it turns out, good things really *do* come to those who wait. My good thing came in the form of a guy named Doug. In my opinion, Doug was the most handsome guy in our first-year medical school class. He was also the kindest, smartest, and most charming. Needless to say, I had the biggest crush on him.

That's when deferring gave way to deciding. After a short courtship, we decided we were both in love. And one night, after talking about our future together over embryology coursework, we decided we should get married and start our family. Our certainty surprised everyone, especially our circles of friends, who would've guessed that each of us would've been the last to get married. But after just six months, we jumped right in with both feet. We got married on my parents' 25th wedding anniversary.

That was just the beginning of the surprises. We welcomed our firstborn son, Sam, while we were still medical students. Unfortunately, we quickly realized that the welcome didn't extend into school. When my mentor heard the news, he said, "Oh, so you're dropping out?" He articulated what everyone was thinking.

I was stunned. No, I had no intention of dropping out. I'd spent my life trying to get into medical school. *Can't I have both?* I thought. I went home and combed through all

Wedding day with Doug in Jamaica

of the handouts and booklets but didn't find any mention of maternity leave. I was scared to ask my mentor about my options. *What if I get kicked out?*

So I didn't say a word and just kept on going. Sam was born on a Thursday, and I was back in class on Monday morning, with Sam strapped tightly to me in a papoose. There was no place to breastfeed, so during a break, I dragged a chair into the bathroom with my foot and nursed him next to the bathroom stalls. And just two weeks after Sam was born, a kind secretary offered to hold him during my first big standardized test. We passed him back and forth as I completed the written portion and standardized patient simulation.

Together, Doug and I resolved that this is what God had in store for us. We were all the more determined to support one another toward our individual and mutual goals. He and I alternated taking one year off to stay home and raise our children while the other completed the very busy clerkships of the third year of medical school.

So I kept right on moving with baby in tow—right into my first business. To make ends meet during my year "off," I began cleaning houses. I hung flyers around school advertising the business as the "Home Medics." At each house, I talked to Sam in his playpen as we moved from room to room, cleaning as we went.

In time, I was pregnant with my daughter, Kendyl, and needed some help with the business. A friend and fellow medical student joined the team. Between the two of us, we made it work. My friend's husband, David, even pitched in

Our children, Sam and Kendyl

and babysat Sam and their two little ones during our really busy days.

A couple of nights a week, I also worked a second job as an educational consultant for Discovery Toys. When Doug returned home, I'd load a bin of stackable cups, blocks, bouncy balls, and pop-up tents into the car and set out to meet groups of mothers. Every month, I advertised the toys by running ads in the newspaper, hanging flyers around school, and setting up booths at festivals and fairs.

Money was still very tight. We diluted milk and took rolls of toilet paper from school. We used food stamps and covered the children with Medicaid until we were finally allowed to add them to our health insurance once in residency.

It was a difficult time, between young children, little money, and a hectic schedule. At school, we also had burned out, unhappy mentors who suffered from compassion fatigue. There were tough patient interactions, and we began to observe the negative patterns of chronic physical and mental illness, addiction, abuse and neglect in the patients we treated. We realized that we were treating one little aspect of larger, global problems. It sometimes made us question our impact in a system that often seemed to support neither the patients nor those trying to provide them care. But it was the career path we had chosen, so we plowed ahead with a desire to make a difference.

Then I got an unbelievable break: I was accepted into a dermatology residency. What makes this unbelievable is that admission into dermatology residencies is among the most competitive. Frankly, I wasn't a very competitive applicant. This is because I didn't initially realize I was interested in dermatology, so I hadn't "groomed" myself like many of the other applicants. But after falling in love with the specialty during a required two-week rotation, I was willing to take the risk. Even more unbelievable is the fact that I had been laser-focused on becoming a pediatrician and had initially considered the required rotation in dermatology a frustrating obstacle.

I'm thankful that I took the risk to apply, and I'm even more thankful that God knows the plans He has for me better than I do myself. I am continually fascinated by the art and science of God's handiwork not only in my own life but in the skin—and the relation between the two. There are beautiful colors, textures, and patterns to be appreciated with God as the master artist and us as His canvas. Through my dermatology residency, I began to understand that skin disease, while most often not life-threatening, affects individuals more significantly than many other ailments. That's because it's visible to the outside world and impacts how people are perceived and treated by others. I began to find such happiness in helping to relieve this suffering.

Somehow, my family and I survived the whirlwind years of medical school, internships, and residencies. It all seemed crazy at the time. Actually, in hindsight, it still seems crazy.

But all things are possible for those who believe, and God did not fail us during this time. I met my husband, who has become such a source of support and encouragement that I cannot imagine life without him. I learned more than any other season of life, though some things I'd like to forget. I came away with a few great friends and wonderful mentors who made the experiences not only bearable, but also enjoyable. And Sam, as he likes to jokingly say, even went through medical school as a baby!

The Missing Piece

> *"I will give them a heart to know me, that I am the LORD.*
> *They will be my people, and I will be their God,*
> *for they will return to me with all their heart."*
>
> – JEREMIAH 24:7

FINALLY! I WAS A DOCTOR!

I'd spent the prime years of my life busy out of my mind in my internship and residency, and now I had arrived at my destination. And the destination looked good. Doug and I were two physicians with good careers, and I was being acknowledged for my professional achievements. We lived in the suburbs in a big house and had nice cars, and our children attended some of the best private schools in the area. From the outside, it looked like we had it all.

But there was a problem.

I didn't feel like I had it all. I felt unsatisfied. I had

Medical school graduation day

arrived at a destination that called for long hours and end-
less physical and emotional demands. The truth was that I
felt drained and unfulfilled.

There was an even deeper problem—one that I should
have seen coming at our graduation, when my medical

22

school class recited the Hippocratic Oath. It includes a provision that says, ". . . respected while I live and remembered with affection thereafter." While the Hippocratic Oath is noble, and this clause is not inherently bad, it can unfortunately become twisted in the minds of some physicians.

You see, in becoming physicians, we had all worked—and continue to work—very hard, giving up much in the process. In time, we come to believe that we should be honored for that dedication. We sometimes put too much emphasis on gaining respect and accolades.

That's what happened to me. I started to become my own god. When I had graduated medical school, I'd thought to myself, *Praise be to God!* But now, several years later, it had slowly and insidiously become, *Praise be to me!*

It happened so gradually that I almost didn't take notice. I was still helping people, but with each new accolade and honor, my focus subtly shifted. I became filled with pride as I looked at my curriculum vitae of nationally and internationally recognized roles. Professor, Director, Chairperson, Principal Investigator, Primary Author, Clinical Scientist, Consultant ... I began to slide down the slippery slope of worldly success, recognition, and approval. Little by little, I gave in, and I didn't seem to mind so much. As I was slowly drawn into the tide, I became immersed in the culture that I thought was focused on altruism, while sadly realizing it was also tainted by bureaucracy, politics, ego, and greed.

Eventually, even the accolades and honors weren't enough to distract me from the fact that there was a problem in my life. I was drowning in all the wrong things. And when I looked into the faces of some of my colleagues, I saw the same disheartened expressions. They were buried under a pile of debt, burned out and feeling a lack of joy, just like me.

It's no wonder. When you start out as a young medical student, you're filled with compassion and an ideal vision of helping heal the sick and assuage their suffering. But then the system can make it nearly impossible to accomplish those goals with so many time-consuming requirements that divert your attention and energy from patient care. You feel like you're fighting an exhausting, uphill battle.

The problem was unbearably noticeable to me one day during a coaching session. It had been recommended that I attend efficiency training because I was spending too much time with my patients. But I felt unsettled. *How can I focus on patient flow that maximizes efficiency—as well as revenue— when a patient just confided that she feels suicidal? Or when a parent of a patient just broke down in tears over a life-changing diagnosis? Or when a patient is scared about an upcoming procedure?* I realized in that moment that I was not going to be efficient at the expense of my conscience. Something needed to change. But what?

I felt as if I was bound in a tight blanket of discontentment and despair from which I could not escape, no matter how much or how hard I struggled against it. *Is it time to walk away from medicine completely?* I wondered. *But I'm still a quarter of a million dollars in debt for my schooling and training! Is there a better way?* I talked to colleagues, attended seminars, met with counselors, and read self-help books. Still I couldn't find the answers I was searching for.

I thought back to the reasons that motivated me to become a physician in the first place, and I realized I had veered way off course. I was distracted by the logistics of medicine. Insurance payments (or lack thereof), prior authorizations, compliance issues, governmental regulations, patient satisfaction scores, electronic medical records, malpractice, schedules, paperwork and more paperwork, decreasing reimbursement, increasing costs, unending administrative and clerical demands . . .

Then I thought about the day I recited the Hippocratic Oath. I had forgotten that God is the only one who should be honored with fame among all men for all time to come. God created this world, including me, and He should be given the glory for all He has done. Instead, I had become entirely too focused on myself. I'd gone into medicine to help children and bring glory to God, but I had sunk to the bottom of my slippery slope. I was called to do more.

It was finally clear what I had to do: re-evaluate my life. And it was finally clear *with whom* I had to do it: God.

We began a diligent search for a church, but months passed and nothing felt right. That is, until one Sunday morning when I knew immediately upon entering the building: *This is it.*

This church had the traditional stained glass windows and pews that Doug liked. And as we were greeted warmly, I was flooded with childhood memories of gathering with other families in my congregation, my parents busy talking with friends while we kids explored our big old church without supervision. I had always felt at home in that church where I had received my spiritual foundation, and I felt at home now.

During the service, I sensed the Holy Spirit there, drawing me back into a relationship with my Savior. Thankfully, God had not given up on me, even though I had wandered far from Him and had a gaping, God-sized hole in His place. I was moved to tears. The hole in my heart slowly started to close.

This is what had been missing.

God's love and acceptance had always been available to me, but I felt it strongly now that I was surrounded by His family. The fellowship of other believers is what I needed to get me back on track. As people reached out to me and welcomed us into their community, the grip of the world slowly seemed to loosen. The blanket of discontentment and despair lifted, and I felt like I could breathe again. This is when things started to fall into place.

Soon afterwards, I was invited to become involved in the Health Cabinet at my church. It was a good fit. I felt connected while also giving back to others. What made it an even better fit was the partnership that developed between this group and another important group for which I was a medical director, The American Academy of Dermatology (AAD)'s Camp Discovery program.

At my first meeting, I told the Health Cabinet about how the AAD sponsors week-long summer camps for children and teens with skin disease. I explained that because it is a national program, campers often fly across the country to attend, but that we struggled to find volunteers to help greet these unaccompanied minors at the airport. The Health Cabinet was looking for ministries to support and was thrilled to become involved. I'd prayed for a solution, and just like that, here was the answer. The AAD Camp would become a permanent ministry of the church.

Meanwhile, another Health Cabinet ministry was starting up, a "First Place 4 Health" Bible study group. "First Place 4 Health" is an amazing, health-focused Bible study that is for everyone, not just those wanting to lose weight. It concentrates on balancing our lives with God at the center. It was a great ministry opportunity for our church members, and they asked for a leader. Almost involuntarily, my hand rose. I said I would do it if someone else agreed to be a co-leader.

As soon as I put down my hand, I froze. *What did you just do?* I thought. *You've never even attended an adult Bible study, and now you're going to lead one? Are you crazy?!*

Luckily for me, my naivety proved to be a blessing. I didn't know what I was supposed to do—or not do—as a Bible study leader, which meant that I didn't have an inflated notion of what I had to live up to as a Bible study teacher. I was free from the weight of comparison as I settled into the new role.

It turned out to be a turning point in my faith. For the first time, I was reading my Bible every day. It was incredible. I discovered the wonderful resource that God left for us here on Earth—a love letter from Him that is so full of rich wisdom and advice for living. I felt closer to God as I drew nearer to Him through His word. And as I began to mature spiritually, I started to crave His Word and all that He had to say to me.

I was ready to listen.

A Purpose and a Promise

"But for this purpose I have raised you up, to show you my power, so that my name may be proclaimed in all the earth."

– EXODUS 9:16

"IT'S NOT ABOUT YOU."

These were the first words that I heard from my CD player one morning on my drive to work. I had finally brushed the dust off an audiobook that I'd bought on an impulse months ago. It was called *The Purpose Driven Life* by a pastor named Rick Warren.[1]

But the first four words didn't sound promising. *What do you mean it's not about me?* I thought, frowning. *I must have bought the wrong book.* I glanced at the cover of the audio

---

1. Rick Warren, *The Purpose Driven Life*, (Michigan: Zondervan on Brilliance Audio, 2017).

book on the passenger seat next to me. The subtitle read, "What on Earth Am I Here For?"

That was the question that had been following me ever since I'd joined a church. As I drew closer to God, I increasingly wanted to do His will for my life. But I had more questions than answers. *What is God's will for me? What path should I take? What am I meant to do?*

I fixed my eyes on the road, barely suppressing my exasperation. *This book is supposed to help me figure out my purpose in life. How could it not be about me?* I thought. But I was desperate for answers, so I turned my attention back to the narrator and resigned myself to listen that day. Then I listened the next day. And the next . . .

I listened to that audiobook for forty days. By the time Rick Warren signed off, something amazing had happened. I grasped a completely new perspective on my life.

You see, when I was younger, I was taught that God had sent His son to die for me. Yes, Jesus came to sacrifice His life so that our sins would be forgiven. God gives us life on Earth with the promise of eternal life through Jesus Christ.

But that is only the first part of the story. There's a second part, and it is this: God expects us to share His story with others so they, too, can know His love and forgiveness and spend eternity with Him.

For the first time in my life, I understood the complete story. I was made *by* Him and *for* Him. And with that understanding, it dawned on me that I was living a selfish life. I wasn't getting the answers I wanted because I wasn't asking the right questions. It's not about what God wants *for* me. It's about what God wants *from* me that will define my purpose in life.

That's when it truly sunk in. *It's not about me.*

These four words were game-changers. I still had that child-like faith, but now I had a grown-up perspective on God in my life. I still wasn't sure in which direction I would accomplish God's purpose, but I knew my life needed to change in big and small ways.

And God was going to help me do that—with His own four game-changing words.

It happened one morning a few months later when I was in the shower, mulling over a decision. For some time, I'd been debating on the high school in which I would enroll Sam. My son was struggling through a very difficult time, and I wanted to make things better for him. But what was the next step? I felt ill-equipped to make this decision, as overwhelmed as the steam that curled around me now and enveloped my body.

I closed my eyes and let hot tears stream down my face. *I'm scared, Lord,* I prayed. *I'm afraid to make a mistake. Please. God, give me direction. Show me the answer.* I pressed my forehead against the wall and began to sob.

"Build a children's house."

These four audible words were unmistakable and undeniable. I quieted, surprised. These were words from God. He had spoken to me in a kind but authoritative voice. I'd read about God speaking to people in the Bible, but did it really still happen today? It wasn't something that had been taught in my church, and it wasn't something that any other believer I knew had experienced or talked about.

But I was certain. I had heard God's voice.

What did it mean? This was not the answer that I was looking for. Build a children's house? What did that have to do with my decision on a high school for Sam? I didn't understand His response. Glancing at the clock, I realized I didn't have much time to think about it. I needed to hurry and get ready for work.

Throughout the day and the rest of that week, I continued to think about what God said. But no matter how many ways I turned it over in my mind, I could not figure out what it meant or what I was supposed to do.

By the end of the week, I still had no idea what He meant. *How can I receive a clear word from God and still be as confused as ever?* I thought in annoyance. I forgot about it for a while, but it never went away completely. God's four words would spring up in my thoughts periodically.

I decided to pray and ask God what He meant by it. After all, He had given more explicit instructions to people in the Bible. I asked Him to do the same for me now. And a few weeks later, He did. I was lying in bed one evening, praying about my children, when I heard His voice again.

"The best is yet to come."

I could hardly move. The words were unmistakable and undeniable, just like I'd heard Him in the shower. This time He spoke with less of an authoritative tone and more with one of reassurance. I did not want that moment to end. An amazing peace that I had never experienced before—and have not experienced since—washed over me.

I thought about His words, marveling at His promise. *The best is yet to come.* I didn't have to struggle or worry about understanding His responses. As I submitted to His purpose for my life, He was preparing to show me His best.

Faith in Action

"But you will receive power when the Holy Spirit comes on you;
and you will be my witnesses in Jerusalem, and in all Judea
and Samaria, and to the ends of the earth."

– ACTS 1:8

C.S. LEWIS ONCE SAID that God uses pain as His mega-
phone.[2] Or as Rick Warren puts it in *The Purpose
Driven Life*, "Your problems are not punishment. They are
a wake-up call from a loving God." In that case, my wake-up
call came one Friday morning at work.

Months after I had heard God's words, my business
manager poked his head into my office.

"Can I talk to you about something?"

2. C.S. Lewis, *The Problem of Pain*, *revised edition*, (California: HarperOne,
2015).

"Sure," I said, glancing at the clock on the wall. We had a few minutes until the next patient.

"It's about your schedule," my business manager began, leaning against the doorway. But as he talked, I felt unsettled. My mind began to shift to a problem that was bigger than the office schedule. Deep down, I knew I was not living the life that God wanted for me. He had given me a clear command and an even clearer promise, and I wanted to do what God was asking of me. At least that's what I had been saying to myself.

The truth was that my words and my actions weren't adding up. I'd read in James 2:17 that "faith by itself, if not accompanied by action, is dead." I said I had faith, but action—real action—required obedience and sacrifice. When it came down to it, these were two things I wasn't very good at. *Not many people like to be told what to do, much less give up what makes them comfortable,* I reasoned with myself. Then another thought followed. *But these things are true of people who make God the singular focus of their lives.*

I had to admit to myself that I was not obedient *or* sacrificial, and this truth was becoming more and more noticeable. In fact, it was becoming unbearable. I'd been praying and crying out to God for direction. I'd pleaded with Him to help me. And in this moment, He did.

As I turned my attention back to my office, I looked at my business manager with a sudden clarity. *I'll never be able take my focus off the things of this world if I don't make some adjustments,* I thought. *I won't be able to listen to what God is calling me to do if I stay here.* This was the proverbial straw that broke the camel's back.

"I quit."

The words popped out of my mouth right then and there, on the spot. There was a moment of stunned silence as the words hung in the air. I was just as shocked as the business manager. Behind him, the nurses bustling in the hallway froze and looked at me.

I managed to collect enough thoughts to tell him to hold off on making any announcements or changes to my schedule. I wanted to be able to talk with the practice owner the following Monday—not to mention that I needed to call my husband during my lunch hour to break the news! Fortunately, Doug was understanding, and not completely surprised. He had watched my private struggle unfold for some time.

That Sunday, I woke up early before going to church to type my resignation letter. As the printer inched out the letter, I stared at the blank space awaiting my signature. *God, would you confirm that I'm doing the right thing?* I asked. He answered me a couple of hours later.

That morning in church, my pastor was giving a sermon about making decisions for Christ. He said, "There may be some of you who are even thinking about quitting your job to follow what you know God wants for you." I sat up, eyes wide. It was as if God was speaking directly to me.

Luke 12:48 came to mind. It says, "From everyone who has been given much, much will be demanded; and from the one who has been entrusted with much, much more will be asked." I had been given and entrusted with much, and now I was convinced that He expected more from the life I was living.

Then I remembered Luke 9:23, in which Jesus said, "Whoever wants to be my disciple must deny themselves and take up their cross daily and follow me." It was time to take up my cross and follow Christ in obedience and sacrifice.

When I returned home from church, I signed the resignation letter. Closing my eyes, I breathed a long sigh of relief. Finally. I was free to focus on God's plans and purposes, to respond to His calls to action. And He wasted no time.

That very same day, an announcement in the church program caught my eye. Our church was accepting applications for an inaugural congregational mission trip to Quebrada de Agua, Guatemala. I was excited. I'd been intrigued by the possibility of going on a mission trip, and this was my opportunity! I applied that day and was accepted.

Things continued to move quickly. That evening, I attended my first formal training class for missions. I knew that it would be helpful but not necessary—all God needed was my willing heart for His purposes. And Jesus promised in Luke 12:12 that "the Holy Spirit will teach you at that time what you should say."

Nonetheless, the class was awesome and eye-opening. It was the first week of a fifteen-week course called *Perspectives on the World Christian Movement*. Its focus was on "how every believer can be intimately woven into the story of God using His people to be a blessing to all the peoples of the earth."

In *Perspectives*, I learned that God is a missionary God who wants to restore a perfect relationship with each and every one of us. Because of His great love for us, He sent His son, Jesus, to fulfill His mission and bring glory to His Father. Jesus came as our Savior so our sins would be forgiven and we would have eternal life.

But He wants us to share that love with others. So in each of the Gospels, Jesus gives His people what is called the "Great Commission." He commissions His people to fulfill His mission in the world by sharing His message of salvation. In Matthew 28:18-20, He said, "Go therefore and make disciples of all the nations, baptizing them in the name of the Father and the Son and the Holy Spirit." And in John 20:21, Jesus said, "Peace be with you! As the Father has sent me, I am sending you."

So the simple command for followers of Christ is twofold. We are to love Him and to love our neighbors as ourselves. This is the "Great Commandment" that Jesus explained in Matthew 22:36-40. And now He explained with the "Great Commission" that we are also to share His message with the world. Unfortunately, Jesus said in Luke 10:2, "The harvest is plentiful, but the workers are few." What is even more unfortunate is that sixty-eight people are dying every minute without knowing Christ as their Savior. This fact broke my heart, but I knew it broke the heart of God even more.

In *The Hole in Our Gospel*, Richard Stearns impressed God's expectation upon me even more. He said, "Any authentic and genuine commitment to Christ will be accompanied by demonstrable evidence of a transformed life."[3] By the end of the course, my life was indeed transformed.

I realized I had the privilege and the honor—and also the command—to be part of the Great Commission. A fire was ignited in me that I wanted to share. I recognized this mission trip as an invitation to join Him in His work, so I gladly accepted the invitation and began packing my bags.

Before I zipped my bags shut, I tucked a copy of my favorite poem into a pocket of a suitcase. It was by Saint Teresa of Ávila.[4]

Christ has no body now but yours.
No hands, no feet on earth but yours.
Yours are the eyes through which He looks
    compassion on this world.
Yours are the feet with which He walks to do good.

---

3. Richard Stearns, *The Hole in Our Gospel: What Does God Expect of Us? The Answer That Changed My Life and Might Just Change the World* (Tennessee: Thomas Nelson, 2010).

4. Saint Teresa of Ávila, "Christ Has No Body But Yours," Catholic Community of St. Francis of Assisi, Raleigh, NC, www.stfrancisraleigh.org/charis/teresa-of-avila-christs-body, accessed August 8, 2017.

Faith in Action

Yours are the hands through which He blesses all
    the world.
Yours are the hands; yours are the feet; yours are the
    eyes; you are His body.
Christ has no body now on earth but yours.

I was ready to go out into the world and do His will.

A World of Similarities

"Consequently, you are no longer foreigners and strangers,
but fellow citizens with God's people and also members of his
household, built on the foundation of the apostles and prophets,
with Christ Jesus himself as the chief cornerstone."

– EPHESIANS 2:19-20

WHEN WE ARE OPEN and available to be used by God, He will waste no time in using us for His good. I discovered this truth first-hand as I was preparing for my first mission trip to Guatemala and realized it wouldn't be my first trip after all. Instead, I was surprised to receive an invitation from a friend to join another short-term mission trip. This trip was to Managua, Nicaragua, and it would begin within the week!

I scrambled to get ready for this trip, even though I didn't know many details. To be honest, I hadn't asked many questions about the trip beforehand. I had not had the chance to meet the team since they were coming from a church in another city. I had no idea where we would be working, what the itinerary looked like, or even where we would be staying.

But I was certain of one thing: As soon as my friend invited me, I felt called to go. In that moment, I was simply trusting God.

A week later, I was filled with a mixture of emotions as I approached the group of twenty other missionaries waiting at the airport gate. Their hearty welcome instantly put me at ease. We fellowshipped briefly and then grabbed a bite to eat before our departure. While I waited in line, I looked down and smiled to myself. Multiple pennies were scattered on the ground.

They reminded me of a chain letter I'd read once. The letter told of a wealthy man who was taking business clients out for dinner. On the way into the fancy restaurant, he saw a penny on the ground and stopped to pick it up. He paused a moment as he looked skyward. This piqued the curiosity of his client, who asked at dinner why a rich man like him would stop for a penny. The rich man replied, "I consider these pennies to be pennies from heaven."

Ever since I'd read that letter, I had developed a special fondness for pennies. These coins represented God-appointed moments for reflection and praise, and they seemed to have an uncanny way of showing up at the perfect time when I needed some encouragement or affirmation.

I bent down and scooped up the pennies around my feet, feeling reassured that I was following the right path. As I settled into my seat on the plane, I squeezed the pennies in my hand and thanked God that we were on our way to Managua, Nicaragua, to share His love and promises with the people there. I was unsure what to expect, but I was filled with anticipation.

Several hours later, we arrived. Our group was whisked through customs before we spilled out of the airport into the hot, sticky night air of Nicaragua. As we boarded a bus, little children crowded around us, holding up their wares of woven reeds for sale. The bus rumbled through the city, past a blur of dirty cars and old buildings with peeling paint. A pervasive scent of sweat drifted into the windows and clung to us along the way.

The next morning, we were served an authentic breakfast of warm tortillas, eggs, and fresh fruit as we prayed, read scripture, and talked excitedly about the plans for that day. Then we went to work at local orphanages and schools, examining kids' skin and performing health screenings until our backs were drenched with sweat.

Afterwards, we delivered food to families in need. A pastor drove us to little, dark adobe houses, where we found families sitting outside in the dirt. They were understandably cautious at first; that is, until we pulled out lollipops, the universal symbol of friendship, which inevitably drew thankful smiles.

Each day began and ended in the same way. The hours were long, and the days were hot. Although the culture was

Our team in Nicaragua

Delivering food in Nicaragua

very different in many ways, I began to discover many similarities.

For example, I realized that the concerns of the children in Nicaragua were the same as those of the children I cared for at home. They wanted treatment for things that were bothersome. They wanted to be reassured that their condition was not serious and that they would be okay. And they wanted care that would help them fit in with the others in their community—just like we all do.

I was especially struck by our similarities one evening during a worship service that we attended with locals. Even though we didn't speak the same language, and didn't have the same worship style, we were unified as brothers and sisters in Christ. As I looked around at all of the people, it was obvious to me that God is working in all of the world and that we are all part of one family.

I stood in reverent awe. Then a song came to mind that I had sung as a child in Sunday school, "He's Got the Whole World in His Hands." Suddenly, the lyrics came to life in my heart; I understood the words with new clarity. This moment of heavenly insight moved me so greatly that I could hardly speak. I simply cried in adoration to our God.

Just then, as if in response to my thoughts, a young girl from the orphanage came over to stand by our group. Her name was Luz, which means light. A huge smile spread across her face, and her eyes truly glistened with the light of Jesus.

I stared at Luz as evidence of God's love—a love so great and powerful that it is poured on His children all around the world through His son, who suffered and died for our sins so that we could spend eternity with Him. This little girl was a glimpse that Jesus is truly among us, that His spirit lives and shines in each one of us when we accept Him as our Savior. What a gift to us—a gift that I had the privilege of sharing with a young woman the next day.

A local woman had a condition that made her skin varied in color. Instead of one uniform color, her skin was a mix of two colors. Her condition is called mosaicism, in reference to mosaic artwork that is made up of unique and variable pieces. In our skin, the genes from our parents typically mix so that they give one evenly-toned color to our skin. But sometimes the genes do not mix completely, and this causes some areas of the skin to express more of the genes from the mom and some areas of the skin to express more of the genes from the dad. This leads to a beautiful pattern of coloration in the skin, though it is not always perceived as beauty by the people who are affected by it.

This was the case with this young woman. She felt ashamed of herself and very self-conscious of her condition. She was even more embarrassed that her daughter had very light skin because that is the gene she passed on to her, which made her daughter stand out from those around her.

Fortunately, a few members of our team had the opportunity to spend time talking with this woman. We shed many tears together as we explained why her skin looked the way it did. I shared with her the fact that her condition showed her connection to both her mother and her father in a visible way for which she could be thankful every time she looked at herself in the mirror. I also reminded her that her skin showed a very special connection to her daughter.

One thing I emphasized was that God does not make mistakes. He loved her dearly. He had created her just the way He wanted, her skin an artful handiwork that only she could claim. Then I took the cross necklace from around my neck and pressed it into her hands, urging her to keep it so that she could remind herself that she was God's masterpiece whenever her faith and knowledge of this faltered. When she left that day, she went away reassured that she was a special child who was loved by her Father.

The young woman was not the only one we touched. By the end of the week, we had collectively evaluated one thousand people who had limited access to medical care, and I had said "Jesús te ama"—which means "Jesus loves you" in Spanish—at least five hundred times. But as I peered out of my airplane window on the flight home, touching the empty spot on my neck where my cross necklace had once been, I knew I had gained even more from my time in Nicaragua than I had given.

A World of Differences

"There are different kinds of gifts, but the same Spirit distributes them. There are different kinds of service, but the same Lord. There are different kinds of working, but in all of them and in everyone it is the same God at work."

– 1 CORINTHIANS 12:4-6

TWO WEEKS AFTER my impromptu trip to Nicaragua, I arrived at the airport again, this time ready to embark on my scheduled trip to Guatemala. When I stepped out of the car, there were five pennies waiting for me on the ground again. I grinned as I slipped the treasures into my pocket, thrilled that this trip was starting on a promising note like last time. But this was where the similarities ended; the trip to Guatemala turned out to be quite different from Nicaragua for several reasons.

For one, I wasn't going with strangers; I was going with

members of my church, and it was our first visit as a congregation. We'd had several planning and preparation meetings before the trip, and although our team had dwindled from ten people to five people, we were an enthusiastic five who were ready to serve and make a difference. As we greeted each other at the airport, I was excited to be able to give each member of our team one of my pennies, thanking God for His encouragement on our endeavor.

Also unlike the last trip, the beginning of our journey was a bit rocky because one of our team members had serious anxiety about the flight. We prayed together from Philippians 4:6-7, which says, "Do not be anxious about anything, but in every situation, by prayer and petition, with thanksgiving, present your requests to God. And the peace of God, which transcends all understanding, will guard your hearts and your minds in Christ Jesus." Several hours later, we landed in Guatemala.

But once we landed, our travel plans *literally* became rocky. We climbed into an old van and bumped along for the next four hours through mountainous terrain. The gears churned loudly as we hugged the side of a mountain, and I squeezed my eyes shut so that I wouldn't look at the drop-off just a few yards away. It felt like we were lurching precariously along the edge of the earth.

We were relieved when we finally arrived at our hostel in Quebrada de Agua, a remote village in the mountains of southern Guatemala. The resident missionary who welcomed us was a blessing. Not only could he sing, play guitar, and speak Spanish, but he was a great example of a person after God's heart. He ushered us to a local restaurant nearby, where our group sat in bright lawn chairs around a table draped with a bright vinyl tablecloth. A plastic basket of warm tortillas was placed in the center of the table, and we were served eggs and fresh fruit.

The next morning, I was excited for what lay ahead. Unfortunately, as we prepared for another ride up the mountain, we found that our old van was no longer functional. It may have been Satan's plan to stop us from advancing God's kingdom, but we were not going to be deterred. I must admit, however, that I had trepidation regarding our safety when I heard about our back-up plan: we were going to ride up the mountain, with its sharp drop-offs and uneven terrain, in the back of an old pickup truck with peeling and faded paint. Fortunately, God gave me the peace I needed to climb into the truck and grind our way up the mountain, passing other trucks along the way that were also crammed full of people.

I knew the grueling journey was worth the effort when the village children rushed to crowd around our truck, greeting us with excited smiles. We were quickly ushered into a church service and welcomed by the congregation. After the service, we had time to interact with the church members before our meeting with the leaders of the community. We also met with the teachers of the school to discuss their ideas for our partnership. It was a reached community in that they had heard the message of the Gospel, but we discovered that they were not filled with the joy of the Gospel. They were hard workers who lived

The pickup truck that brought us up the mountain in Guatemala

tough lives, and their hearts were consumed with concerns about how they would feed their children the next day.

This was another difference between the two mission trips. Unlike the trip to Nicaragua, our purpose here was not to provide medical care; it was to build relationships with these village people. The best part of this mission was going to the school each day and interacting with the children. We read Bible stories, sang songs, and played on the playground with them. It was wonderful to see how hungry the children were for God's Word. They focused intently on the lessons that were being read, and they scooted together tightly to look at the children's Bible. It was encouraging to meet several children in Quebrada de Agua who were receptive to the Gospel message and who were willing to share it with others.

Guatemalan children hungry for the word of God

We also visited with families in the village every afternoon. What a blessing to be able to share fellowship with
them—not only to hear their needs, but also to hear how
God had proven faithful in their lives. One elderly couple
in particular provided living proof that the love of the
Savior provides a light to others. They were exceedingly
warm and welcoming, literally beaming as they told of their
love for one another and for Christ. We shared hugs and
authentic laughter during our visit together, and it was
obvious that they had found something more precious than
gold: they had found a relationship with their Lord. They
were a strong Christian example for their family and their
community—not to mention our team—in the joyful way
they lived their lives despite having limited resources.

The couple in Guatemala whose light shone brightly

Our next family visit provided an unexpected opportunity for my own spiritual growth. We entered a small adobe hut, and I blinked my eyes to adjust to the heat and smoke that filled the hut from the oven. We settled onto woven mats on the dirt floor, and I could see only one small family bed in the bedroom. As we talked with the family, I felt that we should pray with them, so I made the suggestion to one of my team members.

"Good idea," she said, nodding. "You should pray."

I blinked again, not because of the stuffy air but because of what she had just said. *Me? Pray out loud?* I thought, suddenly feeling uncertain. I had never prayed aloud before, but my team gave me strong encouragement now. I didn't have time to think about it longer, because the circle of people in the hut clasped hands and waited for me to speak. I don't remember what I said, but that was the day I overcame my fear of praying out loud—and I wouldn't look back.

The contrast between the two trips wasn't the only difference that I noticed: when we held an impromptu women's Bible study for the women in the village, I also became aware of the differences between each woman. We were giving our testimonies of how God had worked in our lives, and I was amazed to discover the very different life experiences among us all. But I was even more amazed that despite the differences, every testimony revealed the same message: When we put God first in our lives, everything else falls into place. We were so reassured of God's power in each of our lives during this meeting that several of the women were inspired to start their own daily Bible study.

Perhaps the most phenomenal difference of all, however, were the distinctly individual God-given gifts that our team members shared with the people of Quebrada de Aqua. For example, one woman who was meticulous and detail-oriented naturally took on the role of setting our schedule and running our meetings, and a Spanish-speaking teacher dedicated her time to teaching Bible studies to the children and giving sermons to the women. A man with experience in sports ministries spent time repairing basketball nets for the village children, and a Zumba instructor spread the joy of dancing.

And even though I was not in Guatemala to provide medical care, God miraculously found a way to use my expertise anyway. One day, the oldest woman in the village approached me and told me all about a terribly itchy rash she had developed. Her arms were pink and scaly, red in some areas because of her constant scratching. She had no idea I was a physician, let alone a dermatologist! I immediately recognized her rash as a symptom of an allergy to the fragrance in her laundry detergent. Fortunately, we were able to get this woman the medication she needed, and she was already much improved by the end of our trip. My team joked, "You've just expanded your practice!"

I marveled at the "God-incidence" of treating a woman with a skin problem. I call it a "God-incidence" because I don't believe in mere coincidences; I believe that God orchestrates even the smallest details of our lives for His goals. As I prepared to return home, I wondered why my medical knowledge and skills kept resurfacing at a time when I was ready to put my medical career behind me. What I didn't realize is that this was yet another hint that God had other plans for me.

My "patient" in Guatemala

God-Incidences and Answered Prayers

*"And we know that in all things
God works for the good of those who love him,
who have been called according to his purpose."*

– ROMANS 8:28

I HAD EXPERIENCED a whirlwind of new cultures and learning during my trips to Nicaragua and Guatemala, but my rapid-fire adventures weren't over yet. Weeks after I returned home, I received a surprising call about a mission trip to Kenya. I had applied to the trip with the understanding that the waitlist was as long as twelve months, but here I was, already receiving news that I was accepted. I set the phone down in amazement.

I'm going to Kenya! I thought, feeling giddy with excitement. *What an opportunity to see the world! What a chance to help others in need!*

But my excitement soon gave way to uneasiness. Even though I had experienced the other two mission trips, this trip felt different. Nicaragua and Guatemala were only a few hours away from my hometown by plane, but Kenya was more than eight thousand miles away, across the Atlantic Ocean. Not only that, but this was a secular trip; it wasn't coordinated by a faith organization. *Will I be able to pray with patients?* I wondered, and then more questions swirled in my mind. *Is it safe? What if I get sick? What vaccines do I need? Will I be able to communicate with my family? Do they have Diet Coke?*

I packed nervously, wondering if I really was up for this big of an adventure. But before I knew it, I was grabbing my bags and exiting a bus into Kenya, bracing myself for the same hot, dusty air that clung to us on the last two trips. The bus guide smiled at me on my way out. "Welcomes are important here in Kenya," he said. And indeed they were. I stepped out to meet a group of local Kenyans who were singing a traditional welcome song.

Jambo	*Hello*
Jambo bwana	*Hello, sir*
Habari gani?	*How are you?*
Nzuri sana	*Very fine*
Wageni	*Visitors*
Mwakaribishwa	*You're welcome*
Kenya yetu	*Our Kenya*
Hakuna Matata	*There is no problem*

Instantly, the questions and concerns that had been spinning in my head for weeks dissipated in their joyous shouting, chanting, and clapping. I smiled, recognizing the beauty and warmth of God in these people. As their growing chorus encircled us, my eyes drifted to the expanse beyond them, and I was surprised to find an equally beautiful land, lush and green, very different from the dusty harshness of Nicaragua and Guatemala.

We quickly got to work at the Baraka Health Clinic, a simple, well-maintained construction of white cinder blocks. Its name, which is translated as "blessings," was painted in bright, light blue letters across an iron gate at the entrance that led to a beautifully landscaped central courtyard. The clinic was sponsored by a phenomenally social-minded organization called Me to We that also provided clean water, education, and microfinance to those in need. These initiatives were a true blessing for the community, and the community members were all obviously proud of their ability to produce positive change in their lives. This was epitomized in the sayings inscribed on the walls of the clinic, including the reminder that "we are blessed and strengthened and grateful for this day." The clinic staff treated any and all who needed medical help for a nominal fee for visits and medication, in support of "hand-ups, not hand-outs."

While this was a secularly-supported trip, God's work was clearly evident in and around me. I encountered two patients with very rare genetic skin diseases who might

The Baraka Health Clinic in Kenya

have otherwise eluded an accurate diagnosis, had I not researched and written chapters in major dermatology instructional textbooks on these very conditions. One was so rare that it had only been reported a few hundred times in the medical literature, a fact that only made me more certain that this was not of my own doing, nor a coincidence. It was a "God-incidence," a work of God who can do all things and who brought us together according to His plan.

God's work was also evident in an encounter with an adolescent girl who suffered from an unusual blistering disorder. The girl was so devastated by the small pustules covering her neck and creeping up her face behind her ears that she slumped forward, her hood pulled way over her head to protect her from the stares of others. Next to her, her father begged for help for his daughter.

I desperately wanted to provide help, but I was unsure of the girl's diagnosis, and it would be difficult to provide appropriate treatment without a correct diagnosis. She had been evaluated on two previous dermatology trips but had not responded to the treatments she was given for a suspected infection. I did the limited work-up that was available in the clinic, and I did not find evidence of an infection. I consulted with my colleagues, who collectively felt that I should treat her with a stronger medication for a possible infection because infections were so commonplace in the area.

But I remained conflicted. In my heart, I believed the blistering was due to an inflammatory process; the problem was that I had no way to prove it. And if I was wrong and it *was* an infection, the medication that I would prescribe could possibly make it worse.

As I sifted through all of the implications of my next move, a book study came to mind. I was right in the middle of reading *The Workbook of Living Prayer*, by Maxie Dunnam. In it, Dunnam said, "More often than not, God answers your prayers through others, and God answers others' prayers through you."[5] *What a humbling thing that God could allow me to be the answer to someone's prayer*, I thought. Then I took out my notes from the Bible study

---

5. Maxie Dunnam, *The Workbook of Living Prayer* (Tennessee: Upper Room, 1998).

and focused on another sentence: "It is the testimony of people who practice living prayer that things happen when we pray that do not happen when we don't pray."

What an incredible thought, I mused, letting that truth sink in. *'Things happen when we pray that do not happen when we don't pray.'* I closed my eyes and prayed for God to guide my management of this patient. *Use me and our entire team for Your glory, Lord,* I whispered. I also prayed for a record number of patients, especially the opportunity for the birth of a baby in the new maternity ward that was underutilized.

God, in His love and graciousness, answered my prayer right away. I felt certain that I should treat my young patient with medication for an inflammatory condition, not an infection. When she and her father returned at the end of the week for a reevaluation, I was thrilled to see her—and even more thrilled to see that she'd had a positive response to her treatment. All of her blisters were healed! We celebrated ecstatically while she quietly beamed. Even in their stoic society, her father was so moved that he dropped to his knees in tears, blessing me and my family for the care of his daughter. We ended the visit in joyous prayer together to the One who made it possible.

God wasn't finished answering my prayers. Not just one baby was born in the maternity ward that week . . . Healthy twins were delivered into the world! My grin only widened with this new "God-incidence." He also allowed us to treat a record number of patients, including performing skin evaluations on children at a local school and treating them for intestinal parasites. To make the exams

Grateful father and his daughter in Kenya

fun and less frightening, I pointed to each child's belly button and called it by the Swahili term, "mooget," to make the students laugh. And at the end of the exam, I high-fived them and said, "Jesus loves you." They crowded into the classroom for this special blessing.

But the most amazing experience waited until our last day in the clinic, when I saw a two-week-old infant for her follow-up visit. Her mother had walked nearly five miles for the visit with her baby tied to her back. Amazingly, this was not a problem for her because her baby was lighter than the water jugs that she carried from the river five times each day. However, I can attest first-hand at how heavy those water jugs are when they're strapped around your head for miles, because we had walked to get our own water one day.

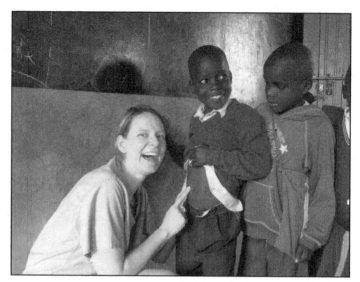

Practicing my Swahili

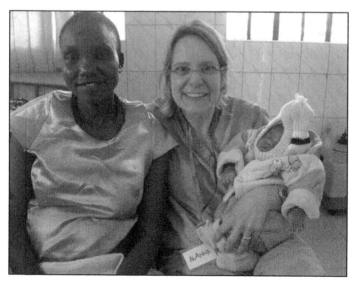

Thankful mother and her baby in Kenya

When the mother and her infant arrived, I saw that the baby's condition was fortunately improving with the treatment that we had given her earlier in the week. Her mother was pleased that the baby was thriving, and all of us in the room—including an interpreter, his daughter, and another missionary—expressed our joy through music. I taught them "Jesus Loves Me" in Spanish with accompanying sign language, which I had learned on my recent trip to Guatemala, and we all sang it together.

Then I asked if they had any traditional Christian songs in their culture that they could teach me. That is when I was introduced to a song called, "There is No God Like You."

Hakuna Mungu kama wewe	*There's no one, there's no one like Jesus*
Hakuna Mungu kama weee	*There's no one, there's no one like Him*
Hakuna Mungu kama wewe	*There's no one, there's no one like Jesus*
Hakuna na hatakuwepo	*There's no one, there's no one like Him*
Nimetembea kote kote	*I've walked and walked all over, over*
Nimezinguka kote kote	*I've turned and turned all over, over*
Nimetafuta kote kote	*I've searched and searched all over, over*
Hakuna na hatakuwepo	*There's no one, there's no one like Him*

As our voices joined together in singing to God, I looked down at the sweet baby in my arms and around at the new friends surrounding me in the small clinic room. I felt content and thankful to be there at that moment, helping others and having my own life blessed in such a personal and impactful way. I was right where God wanted me to be.

Later that evening, we were met with a special surprise when the Baraka Health Clinic staff joined us for our last dinner. We had all enjoyed an incredible, collaborative work environment throughout the week, so they wanted to express their gratitude to us. As was our nightly tradition, we went around the table to share our favorite experience, listening to our team members who had many different faith traditions take turns sharing. When it was my turn, I found it hard to pick just one moment. There had been so many amazing moments.

Finally, I told them about singing, "There Is No God Like You." I asked the team to indulge me by having our colleagues from the Baraka Health Clinic lead us in that song together, and it turned out to be a remarkable experience for all of us. Everyone, no matter his or her faith, stood around the dinner table, singing and dancing and radiating joy.

The next morning, as we were riding on the bus to the airport, I traced a new necklace that was hanging around my neck. It had been given to each member of our team as a thank-you gift by the children at the school. I lifted the charm hanging at the end and inspected it, then realized it was a cross with a heart. Inside, it read "Love Forever." Emotions rushed to the surface, overwhelming me as I fought to hold back tears. What a humbling gift from children who had so little in material possessions to give and were so willing to share. I left Kenya forever touched by the people of that country and by my connection to God.

God at Work in Me

---

*"Each of you should use whatever gift you have received
to serve others, as faithful stewards of God's grace
in its various forms."*

– 1 PETER 4:10

I HAD EXPERIENCED so many dramatic changes in my life already. Not only had I given up my job to follow a desire that God had laid on my heart, but I was still reeling from traveling on three mission trips around the world. It had been six weeks of breathless, intensive spiritual growth. But amid all of those new and unfamiliar situations, ironically it would be the stillness and familiarity of home that would challenge me the most.

When I returned home from Kenya, there was so much to process from the three mission trips. My heart was filled with many emotions, and my mind was filled with even more thoughts. *God, did I honor You in a way that brought You glory?* I wondered. *Did I do enough to help those in need, or could I have done more? Why am I so blessed while others suffer? And how can I be so happy and so sad at the same time?*

As life began to settle into a familiar routine, my unsettled mind turned to contemplate the uncertain future that lie ahead of me. *God, what do you want from me now?* I questioned. *How can I use these experiences moving forward? Can I share these experiences with others? Will they truly understand?*

Without a job or a plan, my mind kept returning to a scripture that had hung on the wall of our dining area in Nicaragua. Printed in bold block letters was Psalm 46:10: "Be still, and know that I am God." *Be still,* I reminded myself, feeling encouraged as I pondered my next step. *Be still, even with concerns and worldly distractions pushing against you.*

Fortunately, it was in this stillness that I came across *Experiencing God,* a book by Henry and Richard Blackaby and Claude King.[6] It served as a spiritual guide for me during this time, helping to humble me before God. As I read through the pages, I took notes on what the authors called "a crisis of belief."

A crisis of belief involves an encounter with God that is God-sized.

It involves an encounter with God that requires faith.

---

6. Blackaby, Henry, Richard Blackaby, Claude King, *Experiencing God* (Tennessee: Lifeway Press, 2007).

*What you do in response to God's invitation reveals what
you believe about God.*
True faith requires action.

As I sat on the brown leather sofa in our living room
and studied my notes, the sun streaming through the window, I realized that I was experiencing my own "crisis of
belief." But it was the authors' next assertions that stunned
me even more.

*It is a turning point, or a fork in the road, that calls for a
decision.*
You must decide what you believe about God.
*How you live your life daily is a testimony of what you
believe about God.*

I stared at these timely words of wisdom from the
authors. It felt like God was sitting right there next to me,
giving me the answers to all the questions I had been asking. It brought tears to my eyes, which were now finally
opened.

I knew I was not the same person that I was before I'd
gone on the mission trips. I was forever changed, and from
that point on, I wanted my testimony and my life to both
point straight to God and His glory.

I came to a startling realization. *My life is my mission
field!* I thought with new clarity. *Everything I do and say is an
opportunity to be a witness to God's saving love through His son,
Jesus. I don't need to wait for tomorrow, when His plan is*

perfectly laid out in my life. I can start right here, right now. This is His plan for my life. This is His plan for everyone's life!

God began to unfold in my heart and mind the plans and answers He had for my life. I was reminded of the steady stream of "God-incidences" that had sprung up in the last six weeks: the encounters with all of the children and the woman with mosaicism in Nicaragua, the woman who sought out my help for her rash in Guatemala, and the children with rare genetic disorders whose paths I crossed in Kenya. These were undoubtedly God-arranged appointments, as evident to me now as the pennies that had winked at me from the ground.

Then I considered all that I had studied and learned in my career, along with all the knowledge and skills that were my God-given gifts. More importantly, I thought about how I would not be able to be used for His glory if I did not put these gifts into practice. I now realized I was divinely called to be a physician caring for children with skin disease, introducing them to Jesus—who could truly change their lives—in the process.

The questions that had cluttered my mind now parted effortlessly to make way for God's plan. It was clear to me now that my desire to walk away from a career in pediatric dermatology and onto new endeavors was not God's plan for me. I had dedicated my life to healing people with His guidance when I was in college, and God was making it obvious that He wanted me to continue to serve Him by continuing in this calling.

What about the children's house you commanded me to build, Lord? I pondered in prayer. He certainly wouldn't have wasted His time speaking to me if He didn't expect me to do something about it. It was a question that beset me during my travels on the mission field in each of the countries I visited.

In that moment, I recognized the answer was right before me. There were so many children and families in my own community with physical, emotional, and spiritual needs that I could help fulfill by simply using the gifts God had given me. As understanding dawned on me, I grabbed my Bible and eagerly flipped the pages until, finally, my finger rested on Esther 4:14. "And who knows," I read, "but that you have come to your royal position for such a time as this?"

God had put me in this place—in this position—for such a time as this. It took a trip across the world (or three) to realize that I was to build a children's house *right where I was.* I closed my eyes as relief and thankfulness washed over me. *Imagine that. I assumed I was going on these trips to help others,* I thought, laughing to myself, *when it was God helping me the whole time!*

Some words drifted to mind from one of my favorite Sunday school songs from childhood, "This Little Light of Mine."[7]

---

7. Harry Dixon Loes, "This Little Light of Mine," Lyrics Mode, http:// www.lyricsmode.com/lyrics/r/religious_music/this_little_light_of_ mine.html, accessed September 5, 2017.

A Children's House

This little light of mine,
I'm gonna let it shine.
This little light of mine,
I'm gonna let it shine.

Let it shine, let it shine, let it shine.

Hide it under a bushel? No!
I'm gonna let it shine.
Hide it under a bushel? No!
I'm gonna let it shine.

I closed my Bible and stood up, feeling committed. If I was going to return to practicing pediatric dermatology, I would do things differently this time. I would no longer be hiding my light under a bushel. I was going to let it shine—but only for His glory!

A Wrong Turn in the Right Direction

"Blessed rather are those who
hear the word of God and obey it."

– LUKE 11:28

"WHEN YOU TAKE one step closer to God," my guide in Kenya had told me, "He will take ninety-nine steps closer to you." It was an old saying that she'd learned from her father, and I cherished her words now. I was not certain in which direction God wanted me to take my first step. That's why it's so ironic that it would be a wrong turn that would land me smack in the middle of God's plan.

But I didn't know that yet when I woke up early one morning to take my first step. I had pulled my computer onto my lap and searched, "Christian doctors Houston." If I was going to practice pediatric dermatology differently, then I figured I would start by connecting with other physicians striving to integrate their faith in their work-place. It didn't take long for my search to produce an organization called the Christian Medical and Dental Associations (CMDA).

It was refreshing to find other like-minded individuals with a focus on Christ before all else—and with an understanding of the sacrifices of the medical profession. Through my involvement with CMDA and another group, Oasis Medical Fellowship, I was mentored and began mentoring others on the Christian walk within the medical profession. We learned from each other's experiences to incorporate faith into our practices, helping to keep them in perspective in relationship to our Father's sacrifice for us.

I also came across another resource to guide me in honoring God through my work as a physician: a book by Dr. Gene Rudd and Dr. Al Weir called *Practice by the Book*. I had not studied it in medical school or residency, but it was one that had vital knowledge for working and serving as a physician in a world that is suffering. It was an encouragement and a reminder that "our vocation as doctors is to open our hearts to the vision of God's love in the world." And this is exactly what I planned to do. I knew this was where God was leading me, and I knew I needed to listen intently to His leadership so my efforts would not be misguided.

Pointed in God's direction and armed with these resources, I was ready to lay the foundation for my new practice. It was going to be something unique, something special, and something only God could do through me. I wanted to renovate a house to give a warm and inviting feel to my office, a place where I could not only share my medical expertise, but also my love and support. I wanted people to feel welcome, like they were coming into my home when they came for an appointment. And I wanted to name it "A Children's House for Pediatric Dermatology." *The ultimate God-incidence,* I thought to myself, smiling. I began looking at houses for sale in the city.

As God's plans for me began to take shape in my mind, I realized that I would need to treat so much more than just the physical aspect of skin disease and birthmarks. I would also need to treat the significant social, emotional, and spiritual aspects that are often of far greater significance for individuals and families than the skin conditions themselves.

This point had been reinforced every summer when I volunteered for the AAD's Camp Discovery, a place where children affected with life-altering skin conditions can be themselves, away from the stares of others in the world who focus on outer beauty. For more than seventeen years, I'd been blessed to work with many amazing colleagues at the camp, watching the transformation of countless lives. And each year, the comments from the campers were the same. "I wish this didn't have to end," they all said.

Now, as I considered my new practice, I wondered, *Well, why does it have to end? Why can't the positive experiences be recreated and spread throughout the year to involve even more children? And why can't these experiences be extended to parents and siblings who also need support?*

A Children's House

An idea for a nonprofit sprouted in my mind alongside my practice. It would be called "A Children's House for the Soul," and it would address these social and emotional issues of living with a skin disease or birthmark. It would empower children to truly love the skin they're in, appreciating that their true beauty is not based on their outward appearance, but on the person inside. The program would also allow children and families to meet with others in the same situation, helping them realize that they are not alone. Fortunately, we are never alone if we have God in our lives; thus, a Biblical component would be offered to help care for the spiritual needs of those who wished to join in.

I was excited about the plans that were developing in prayer and faithfulness, but there was still a nagging in my heart. Ever since taking the *Perspectives* course, I knew God wanted me to share what I had learned with my own church family. We needed a change in focus—a change in perspective—regarding our role in furthering God's Kingdom through mission. I didn't feel equipped on my own for what I knew He was asking me to do, but despite my uncertainty, I reached out to the pastors at my church. I knew God would give me what was necessary to succeed.

When I impressed this upon the hearts of my pastors and the leaders of our church, they graciously agreed this was important. They asked me to consult with a woman in charge of our adult Bible study classes so we could begin offering a missions-focused Bible study. The day I met with her, we scheduled a new study of *A Hole in The Gospel,* with me as the leader. I was nervous to lead this study, as I wasn't a Biblical scholar, but I did know what God expected of us, and this was a message I was willing to share.

On the way home, I thought about my first steps in God's direction. I was elated to be offering up my life to be used by God. Lost in thought, I took a wrong turn that took me on an unfamiliar route, where I drove past a "For Sale" sign. Suddenly, I was captured by the house behind the sign. Craning my neck in awe, I sharply turned my steering wheel just in time to avoid crashing into a parked car.

I pulled over and sat, eyes wide, staring. *I can't believe it,* I thought, stunned. The brick bungalow perched on the corner was surrounded by trees and had a wrap-around porch and beautiful archways.

I knew instantly that this was the house I had envisioned. *This* was A Children's House.

I looked around at the street in surprise and thought, *I didn't even know houses were available here.* I had been searching for houses in a different part of the city, but with one wrong turn, God had revealed the right house to me. *This house would never have been revealed to me if I had not chosen to be obedient to God,* I realized, shaking my head in wonder. Just like that, God had taken ninety-nine steps closer to me.

Mountain of Obstacles

"I have told you these things, so that in me you may have peace.
In this world you will have trouble.
But take heart! I have overcome the world."

– JOHN 16:33

"**T**HIS HOUSE IS currently under contract."

I blinked at the words on my computer screen, shaking my head, *No, no, no . . . It's only been a week since the house was put on the market! How is it already under contract?* I thought in dismay. I tried to blink the words away, but they continued to stare stubbornly back at me.

Closing my computer, I sagged like a disobedient child, feeling ashamed. I had been attending a Bible study of Gideon by Priscilla Shirer, and through that study, I recognized that I was only partially obeying God in many areas of my life. I prayed, *Father, forgive me for my disobedience. You presented me with the perfect location to carry out Your will, but I allowed the busyness of life to creep in, letting the house slip away.*

But the house wasn't gone yet. That weekend, I received an incredible second chance. I was telling a realtor friend about "the perfect house that got away" when he made a quick call to the listing agent to check on its status. To my astonishment, we learned that the current contract on the house had just fallen through only minutes before! The house was about to be actively listed again.

A closed door was opened, and this time I was definitely going to walk through it. In fact, I scheduled an appointment to walk through it the very next morning. And as soon as I entered the house, I loved it! I could already picture the children playing in what would be the waiting room, and I could imagine providing care in the areas that would become exams rooms.

But it was when I walked outside that I was truly won over. As I admired the brick exterior, I noticed a unique detail that was set between the bricks. Peering closer, I realized the detail was a small cross. I stepped back and saw that the house was covered in small crosses on all sides! *Lord, is this another of your God-incidences?* I laughed to myself. The deal was sealed.

The next day, when Doug was able to come see the house, our realtor let us know that there had been more than sixty phone calls regarding the property in less than forty-eight hours. He strongly advised us to make an offer if we were interested.

Doug and I looked at each other, both knowing that it seemed illogical that we should embark on this journey. Not only did we have very limited business knowledge; we had even more limited funds because I had not been working. But we both knew it was the right decision. A relevant quote from Martin Luther King Jr. came to mind. He once said, "Faith is taking the first step even when you don't see the whole staircase." Even with little resources, we had faith to take the next step. We made an offer on the house that evening, and it was accepted!

Then we turned our attention to the only caveat: We had only thirty days to close on the home. There was a lot to be done in one month, so I rolled up my sleeves, thinking, *it's happening! I'm this close to fulfilling the dream that God laid on my heart!*

I thought the biggest problem had been overcome; after all, my bid for the home had been accepted amid overwhelming interest from other prospective buyers. But I was sorely unprepared for the reality that lie ahead. I was about to face a mountain of obstacles that stood between me and A Children's House, beginning with my first call to my banker.

"You need to get together a business plan and a proforma to be considered for a loan," instructed my banker.

"A business plan and a *what?*" I asked in confusion. This was definitely going to involve a steep learning curve. My banker was a wonderful man who had been a great advisor over the years, so I knew I could trust his direction.

I also knew I would need a lot of help, so my next call was to a friend, a very kind and helpful man who is a certified public accountant. Together with Doug, we hammered out the details of a business plan and a proforma. I was relieved to learn that a proforma is a fancy name for a projected budget.

However, my relief was short-lived. After getting all of the documents prepared, my computer crashed. I lost everything. Feeling incredibly discouraged, I began the process of restoring my hard drive.

In the meantime, I turned my attention to the next step: filing the formation documents to make the business entity official. But this was an obstacle too: we discovered that a version of the business name was already taken. Even worse, the company that had registered the name was no longer open, so we had no way of requesting permission for use of the name. *Oh God, my heart is set on "A Children's House,"* I thought sadly. *I can't imagine naming the practice anything other than the name that You've inspired.* We decided to move forward with the paperwork in hopes that we would find some way to make it work.

Finally, all of the paperwork was complete. Eagerly gathering everything together, I faced yet another wall: there was a government shutdown the very same day that prevented many critical transactions needed for this process to move forward. I couldn't believe it. The number and complexity of the roadblocks popping up at every turn were almost too incredible. They seemed insurmountable regardless of my efforts.

But the obstacles only worsened, which I discovered when I filed an application with the Property Owners Association to request a variance from the deed restrictions that prevented commercial property in the neighborhood. My realtor and I showed up to the president's office to turn in our application and plead our case, but the office administrator explained that the decision process required a sixty-day period for review. *Sixty days!* I wailed privately. *But I only have thirty days to close!* The administrator was polite and professional, so I tried to remain calm in spite of the hopelessness and panic rising inside of me. *God,* I prayed, *I ask that You soften their hearts to the situation so that the board would give their approval quickly.*

The Property Owners Association also raised a concern about the appearance of the business signage that I was going to display on the property. I had no idea what I planned to do with the signage and was uncertain who could help me in such a short amount of time.

I trudged forward to the next item on my to-do list: collecting bids from several contractors for the renovations that would transform the house into a practice. I knew my limited budget would pose a problem, and my suspicions were confirmed when I received my first quote. It was three times greater than my budget for renovations and start-up costs. And with each new quote that trickled in, I became increasingly discouraged.

Doubt crept in, and I began to question myself. *Am I doing my will, or the will of my Father?* I asked myself. *Is this my dream that I was asking Him to bless, or His plan that He had ordained for me?* I truly wanted to dedicate myself to doing what God wanted me to do, but maybe this wasn't it.

Continuing in prayer, I decided to attempt the last task: gathering 20 percent of the cost of the house as a down payment, which we did not have. My banker was supportive and helpful to the best of his ability, but he was required to comply with this loan regulation. Our only option was to liquidate some stock that we had purchased in the local hospital where Doug worked, so I spoke with the CEO of the hospital about our options. He said he would help by initiating the process to release our stock certificate. But when I didn't hear back from him, I learned tragic news: within a five-day period, he had suffered a traumatic injury, underwent surgery, and died suddenly from complications after returning home.

After the hospital returned to transacting business after the tragedy, and still reeling from the shocking news, we resumed the process of releasing the certificate. Unfortunately, it proved difficult to find anyone who would accept it for trading. After calling seventeen brokerage firms, I was ready to give up. Luckily, I was compelled to make the eighteenth call, and they were willing to accept it. But it would take weeks for the certificate to be available for trading—well past our closing deadline.

It was just a little over a week until the deadline for closing, and regrettably, nothing had come together. I did not have a business entity approval or approval from the Property Owners Association. I did not have an affordable contractor or a stock certificate. I certainly did not have a down payment. The only thing I *did* have was a completed inspection report that identified what seemed like a million things that needed to be addressed.

I tried to collect my thoughts into prayer, but I felt hopeless. Breaking down, I sobbed, "God, help me!"

And then just when it seemed the situation could not get any worse, I received a crushing call from my realtor. There was a cash offer on the house that the seller would accept if we could not close on time. *There goes our back-up plan of asking for an extension on the closing,* I thought, hanging up the phone and crumpling helplessly under the weight of this final obstacle.

"Father," I cried, closing my eyes in resignation, "help me know beyond a shadow of a doubt that this is Your will."

And with the next phone call, He did.

Closing Day

"Jesus looked at them and said,
'With man this is impossible,
but with God all things are possible.'"

– MATTHEW 19:26

ONE WEEK FROM CLOSING, I was exhausted and empty-handed. I had nothing to show for my efforts except the clear understanding that this was God's will. But according to Christian theologian J. I. Packer, this was enough. In his classic book, *Knowing God,* he wrote, "Once you become aware that the main business that you are here for is to know God, most of life's problems fall into place of their own accord."[8] Packer was onto something, because I was about to see some problems fall into place.

---

8. J. I. Packer, *Knowing God* (Illinois: InterVarsity Press, 1993).

Moments later, the phone rang. It was a contractor from a company called pHd Construction. *Just another contractor I probably can't afford,* I sighed to myself, mustering the energy to schedule a meeting with him at the house to get his quote.

When he heard that I was a Christian physician, his voice seemed to curl into a smile. "We're going to get along just fine," he said.

I hung up the phone and grabbed my keys. *The way things are going, I may not have time to find out,* I thought, feeling the panic rising again. *Father, give me the strength and faith to fully trust You in all things, no matter how bleak things look.*

At the house, the contractor barely said hello before I ushered him from room to room, hastily explaining my vision for remodeling. It was the same vision I had explained to all of the other contractors. After the short tour, I twirled to face him and said, "I really need your quote so I can ensure you can do this within my budget."

He smiled at me in the same calm, reassuring way that he had spoken on the phone. "Be still, and know that I am Lord," he said, quoting Psalm 46:10.

I stilled, looking at him in surprise. It was the same encouraging quote that had hung in the dining room in Nicaragua, and it was exactly what I needed to hear in this moment.

The contractor explained that the name of his company, pHd Construction, stood for "praising Him daily" and that he, too, had been involved in mission work. "I know that A Children's House is a God-ordained project and that this is the right house for you," he said firmly, then continued, "I'm certain things will fall into place, so keep moving forward. I promise I'll find a way to make this work within your budget. I'm on your side."

I gaped at him, scarcely believing my ears. As I drove away after the meeting, all I could do was cry tears of joy. I wasn't sure how I had found pHd Construction, but I was certain it involved heavenly intervention because God had answered my prayer in a big way!

But God wasn't done. Within the hour, everything else miraculously began falling into place. I received an email from my CPA with news that he had found a way for my business name to be approved. I received another email from the hospital letting me know that I could pick up the stock certificate that afternoon. Then I received an unexpected message from the mother of a previous patient informing me that she was working for a corporate branding company in case I ever needed their services. I skimmed down the list of services and spotted 'business signage.' Perfect timing! I met with her and the owner of the company, and they provided excellent ideas and guidance on moving forward with signage and branding, including the logo and website for my new business that was finally coming closer to becoming a reality.

Then at the first session of my Bible study class that Sunday, a woman whom I'd met in a previous study told me that she had just been elected to her neighborhood Property Owners Association—and that she had reviewed my application at her first meeting! Not only was this woman on the board, but I discovered that a parent of one of my prior patients was also a board member. What were the chances that two people on the neighborhood board would know me and be able to attest to my professional character and integrity? I had prayed that God would put the right people in place to make things happen, and He certainly did. Shortly afterward, I received an email from the president of the Property Owners Association informing me that my application for the variance was approved!

The items on my to-do list were checking themselves off one by one until only one item remained: the down payment. When my banker called to check on the status of the stock certificate, I told him I was picking it up that afternoon and would overnight it to the brokerage firm. He became flustered, certain that we would likely not have funding by our deadline. Later that afternoon, he called to suggest that I sell the stock through the hospital to speed up the process. Then he called again on his way home from his personal cell phone to tell me that he needed to find a way to make this work and that he would talk to me in the morning. The next morning, my banker found a way to creatively fund the down payment while still complying with all of his requirements.

Everything was in place! Feeling both excited and nervous, I was all set to go for the next day. Closing day! All of my roadblocks had been miraculously removed.

But contrary to what I thought, my down payment was *not* the final roadblock. In fact, the final roadblock would seem less like a block and more like an opportunity.

Closing Day

It presented itself one morning when the phone rang while I was organizing the paperwork for the closing. It was the director of pediatric dermatology at the local children's hospital, a colleague and friend whom I respect and admire. The last time we had talked was a couple of months ago, when she had asked me if I'd consider returning to work at the children's hospital. At that time, I told her I was pursuing the plan for A Children's House but said she was welcome to put together an offer if she was serious.

Man, it turns out that she was serious! She was calling to make a verbal offer for employment, and it was an attractive offer indeed. I wasn't sure what to say or think; I hadn't expected her to actually pull it off. It's unheard of to put together a contract offer within one month in a large hospital these days, but somehow, she had done it.

Within a couple of hours, I was with the CFO and Nursing Director at a new satellite hospital where I would be hired to start up pediatric dermatology clinics. It was very impressive, including a lovely chapel, and the administrators were making a hard sell. As we approached the nurse's station in the clinic area, a physician ran up and hugged me. She had been a resident when I was working at the main hospital and told me excitedly that she had requested that I be recruited for this position.

Before I could respond, she continued excitedly. "I've just come from evaluating a patient with a skin problem, and I literally *just* told the patient's mother I wished they could see you!" I could hardly believe it, but her story was confirmed when she pulled me into the exam room and introduced me to the patient and his mother. When we emerged from the room, the nurse said, "We have been praying that you would come here." I was speechless.

As we wrapped up the visit, the Nursing Director asked if I had any questions. She was aware of my tight timeline and alternate plans. One thought bubbled in my mind, and I hesitated for a moment before deciding it was worth inquiring.

"Do you think I would be able to hold support sessions and Bible studies?" I asked, thinking of the emotional and spiritual support I was planning to provide at A Children's House. She said she was unsure but would get me an answer by morning.

I walked to my car, overwhelmed with questions. *Was this the opportunity I was to pursue? Would it help me interact with more patients? Would it help me impact more medical students and residents?* I frowned in concern. *Or is this a test? A potential stumbling block in the plans that God has laid out for me?*

It was a very long night. Doug and I stayed up until the early morning hours, carefully examining and re-examining the pros and cons of each option. But after our discussion, I decided to toss out my logical lists. *This is not about the pros or cons,* I realized. *This is about what God wants.* Crumpling my paper, I dropped to my knees and prayed fervently for an answer until falling soundly asleep.

When I awoke the next morning, I glanced at the alarm clock. The closing was scheduled for three o'clock that afternoon, and I still had not made a decision, so I called the hospital administrator and asked if she had any news about my desire to hold Bible studies and support sessions.

"Yes, I've obtained permission for you to hold the support sessions," she said, "*but* the request to hold the Bible studies was denied."

But. With that one word, God spoke to my heart, providing the answer I needed. This was such a good offer and held so many positive opportunities, including working with people I deeply respected. *But* I knew that I would not be able to effectively do His work the way He wanted me to do it.

This opportunity was not for me. I felt God beckoning me toward A Children's House.

As I drove to the bank to sign the loan paperwork so the funds could be wired to the closing company, I talked and cried about the situation with Jennifer, my dear friend who had helped with the cleaning business while we were in medical school. She agreed that A Children's House did not make sense from a worldly perspective, but she also sensed that it was the right thing to do. The poor assistant at the bank must have thought I was crazy as I sat there, crying and signing the paperwork.

At the scheduled time, I headed out to meet Doug at the closing company in a suburb about thirty minutes away, picking up my children from school along the way. It was a big step, and I wanted my family to be a part of the occasion. But when we arrived, the reception area was empty, and a woman behind a desk looked up at us in surprise.

"Hello? Who are you here to see?" she eyed us curiously.

"We're here for our closing?" I responded, more as a question, sensing that something was wrong. The woman nervously began making phone calls as Doug and I looked at each other with uncertainty. I called my realtor, who assured me that he was on his way.

When she hung up the phone, the woman explained, "As a courtesy to you, the closing was scheduled in an office in the city. The closing agent is there now." I groaned inwardly, thinking, *that location is only five minutes from our home.* The woman continued, "But the agent is on her way here, so sit tight. It's rush hour on a Friday and it's raining, so it'll take her a while."

The minutes crept by as we awaited the agent, and my fears and anxieties seemed to close in on me in the small waiting room. It had been a tumultuous journey to this point, full of obstacles and doubts and questions at every turn, and I still had unsettling doubts that started to flood into my mind. *Is this final step of waiting another test?* I asked myself, *or is it a sign that this is not the right course?*

I stepped outside to catch my breath and clear my head. *God, please help calm me and clear my anxious thoughts,* I prayed desperately. *I need Your reassurance!*

In that moment, I looked up into the sky and halted. There, stretching wide across the sky, was a rainbow. God had shown up for me in His perfect timing. My eyes flooded with tears, and my fears instantly melted away.

As I returned to my seat in the waiting room, I thought about all of the times I had seen God at work throughout

God's reassurance on closing day

my life, making possible the impossible, proving time and again that He is a patient and loving God. Along the way, He had nurtured this fledgling mustard seed of my faith, whispering the promise of A Children's House, a promise that was bigger and better than anything I could have planned for myself. He had encouraged me with His daily miracles, and now this simple sign in the sky beamed peace and reassurance upon me, signaling that it was time to fulfill His promises. I was reminded of Luke 1:37: "For no word of God will ever fail."

When the agent finally arrived, I nearly ran into the conference room. Surrounded by my family in leather chairs around the long formal table, I looked down at the bold signature line waiting at the bottom of the closing document. God had moved mountains for me, but this moment was the mustard seed that He was expecting of me. Twisting my pen open with excited anticipation for what God would do next, I scrawled my name—and took a leap of faith.

Epilogue

---

*"For I am convinced that neither death nor life, neither
angels nor demons, neither the present nor the future, nor any
powers, neither height nor depth, nor anything else in all
creation, will be able to separate us from the love of God
that is in Christ Jesus our Lord."*

– ROMANS 8:38-39

MANY GOOD THINGS have happened since that closing day. Eighteen months after beginning the permitting process, we received the green light to begin the renovations. Then six months later, we held our Open House. And what a joyous day it was!

I've stepped into my roles as a business owner of *A Children's House for Pediatric Dermatology* and a nonprofit executive director of *A Children's House for the Soul*—roles of which I am capable only because of God and His work

Ribbon cutting at our open house

through me. I have also been honored to have led a Missions Ministry Action Team at my church, which has allowed me to study His word more deeply and to mature spiritually.

But to say these years since the closing have been easy would be an utter lie. Many difficult things have happened, like when Doug and I drained our savings and withdrew all of my retirement funds to keep things afloat during the permitting process. Or when we listed the house we purchased for the office on the market for a few days when our doubts got the best of us. The devil has worked hard to thwart our plans, and I am ashamed to admit that I've almost let him.

Not only have I encountered attacks on the business front, but my family has also suffered during this time. At the age of 36, my sister, a mother of two young children,

Sign lighting with our friends and board members

was diagnosed with a very rare stage IV sarcoma, which she is battling to this day. My husband had a freak injury that required surgery and extensive rehabilitation. My son was struggling with severe depression while at college and had to return home, and my daughter was diagnosed with a life-altering chronic auto inflammatory disorder. My mother had a complication during her open-heart surgery and almost died on the operating room table, causing a temporary brain injury. My beloved first dog died of metastatic cancer.

Add to all of that our house issues—including repairing cars, replacing two air conditioning units, and fixing major plumbing issues—and there have been months when there is barely enough money to pay the business mortgage or make payroll. Some moments have seemed more than I can bear. There have been times when I have felt crushed by the weight of it all.

From under the weight of my own professional and personal hardships, I've been acutely aware that pain is universal—it is everywhere in this world. This fact was never more obvious than on my next two mission trips, this time to Tanzania with a missional organization called e3 Partners. I left for the most recent trip a couple of weeks before our property taxes were due, and I had no idea where this money would come from because Doug and I had exhausted both of our personal and business cash reserves and had been turned down for an additional extension on our credit line. To make matters worse, I knew my absence from A Children's House would mean lost revenue.

But I also knew I was being called to this African country because of the divine way in which I had been invited. A medical mission team had been praying for a pediatric dermatologist when one of their flights was cancelled and re-routed to Kenya for a connecting flight—the same flight I was on during my trip to Kenya. Among hundreds of passengers, one of their team members sat next to a member of my Kenyan team, who told them about me and introduced us once we landed. I simply couldn't deny the divine nature of our meeting, so I packed for the week-long trip, praying that God would help.

In Tanzania, our small but mighty medical team of four, along with our fearless leader and Tanzanian colleagues, provided care at orphanages and a medical clinic for nearly 250 children and adults with albinism. Albinism is a genetic condition that causes people to be born without pigment to their skin, hair or eyes. It can lead to blindness as well as fatal skin cancers, which is why ninety-five of the patients were treated with surgical procedures for skin cancers and liquid nitrogen for precancerous skin lesions.

Unfortunately, albinism is a major problem in Tanzania due to the lack of education on sun protection and the limited number of physicians available to treat their skin cancers. Of the one in 2,000 Tanzanians affected by albinism, less than 10% will reach age thirty, and less than 2% will survive to age forty.

But albinism is a major problem for another reason: there is much misconception and false information about this genetic disorder. Sadly, many children with albinism are placed in orphanages in an effort to protect them. This is because their body parts are thought to have special

Our team at one of the Tanzanian orphanages

powers by local witch doctors. Tragically, they are hunted, mutilated, and even murdered so that their body parts can be trafficked. The situation is improving thanks to the passionate work of many, but these children are still often forgotten and forsaken.

On the return flight for that trip, I thought about all of the suffering back in Tanzania and the financial uncertainty that awaited me at home. Why does a loving, benevolent

Tanzanian children with albinism

God allow such tragedies and problems to occur in our world?

I don't profess to have all the answers, but I truly believe in the depths of my soul that God's ways are greater than my ways and that He works all things together for good. While we often have such a narrow worldview, God sees the big picture—the *really* big picture. If He can create the vast array of the cosmos and put together the intricate molecular details to bring about life, I have no doubt that He has a plan for our lives too, even amidst tragedies and problems. And I know that this fallen world is not our true home, so it is good to be a bit homesick for our home in heaven.

I also know that God continues to weave my small life into His "big picture" story. During my flight, He allowed for a fortuitous meeting with the Director General of the Tanzanian Commission for Science and Technology. We were able to share information about the high prevalence and impact of albinism in Tanzania, the difficulties of accessing medical and dermatologic care and sunscreen in the community, and the vital need for education of those with albinism regarding sun protection and preventative care to limit the development of skin cancers.

And we were personally invited to collaborate in raising awareness and to assist in developing a program with local Tanzanians to address the needs of people with albinism.

Another fortuitous event waited for me when I arrived home, one that is still hard for Doug and me to believe, but which is absolutely true. The day before our property tax payment was due, Doug received a bonus, which he was told unequivocally was not going to happen at the end of the year. And when it did happen, the bonus covered our property taxes to nearly the exact penny.

When I reflect on that incredible day and all of the other days since opening A Children's House, I am continually amazed that I serve a God who knows the number of the "very hairs of my head" (Luke 12:7) and who provides for all my needs according to His will. My faith has been refined and strengthened during these years of testing, and for that I am grateful.

In fact, I have been blessed beyond measure *because of these trials*. I've learned to remain faithful to God because He has promised—and proven—that He is with me every step of the way. I've learned some patience, to turn my heart and mind to Him to find the peace and reassurance that I need. And, most of all, I've learned that joy does not come from the world or what it has to offer; it comes from Him alone, through His grace and mercy.

And so, despite not being able to take a paycheck because the revenue has been used to cover the overhead of the practice and the nonprofit, I have never been more content. I've found that when it comes to suffering and joy, James 1:2-4 is true: "Consider it pure joy, my brothers and sisters, whenever you face trials of many kinds, because you know that the testing of your faith produces perseverance. Let perseverance finish its work so that you may be mature and complete, not lacking anything."

Epilogue

Looking ahead, I know that it is my God-given call as a follower of Christ to help others know Him. After all, if I had the cure for cancer, I certainly would not hesitate to share it with others. Why then, if I have a cure that is even better, would I not share it with everyone I meet through my words and my actions? Christ is the most precious gift that I can ever share, and I am humbled by the opportunity to introduce others to Him and His life-changing gift of eternal life.

That is why it is my immense honor to share my God-given faith and gifts through mission work and A Children's House for as long as God allows. It is my great privilege that He continues to use a lowly sinner like me for His purposes, providing medical, social, emotional, and spiritual support to children with skin disorders and birthmarks.

So, as I move forward, I will continue to give God thanks and praise for all that He has done. It is with great anticipation that I look forward to the future that God has planned for me, and I pray that I live each day to the fullest for His glory. As the saying goes in Swahili, "Leo ni leo," which means, "Today is the day." May we live every day like *today is the day*, a gift to be unwrapped and savored together.

To Him be all the glory and praise!

A Letter to the Reader

DEAR READER,
    I feel so blessed to be able to share my story with you. I hope you have been inspired by my testimony and that your faith has been strengthened by reading about the miracles God has done in my life. Even if I have only shared a drop of water or a mustard seed with you, I trust that God can grow it into something more with His glorious, unlimited resources, empowering you with inner strength through His Spirit.

Matthew 5:16 says, "It is my wish that my light will shine before you, that you may see my good works, and glorify my Father who is in Heaven." I pray that you are continually filled by His presence in your life and constantly surrounded by His miracles as you, too, let your light shine for all to see.

If you have not accepted Jesus in your life, I encourage you to invite His miraculous presence now. When You trust Christ to make His home in your heart, your roots will grow down into God's love and keep you strong. Only then will you have the power to understand, as all God's people should, how wide, how long, how high, and how deep His love is (Ephesians 3:17-19).

Allow me to share a prayer of salvation with you:[9]

Dear Jesus,

I need You in my life. I acknowledge that I have sinned, and I come to You right now confessing that and asking Your forgiveness.

Thank You for dying on the cross for my sins. I believe You are the Son of God and that You rose from the dead and are alive today.

I open the door of my heart and receive You as my Savior and Lord. Thank You for forgiving my sins and giving me eternal life. Please take control of my life from here forward and make me the kind of person you want me to be.

In Jesus' name I pray,
Amen.

May you experience the great love of Christ so that you are made complete with all the fullness of life and power that comes from God. Through His mighty power at

---

9. From Jentezen Franklin Media Ministries, https://www.jentezen-franklin.org, accessed October 6, 2017.

work within us, God is capable of accomplishing infinitely more than we might ask or think (Ephesians 3:20).

Join me and all generations as we move forward in God's plan and timing, clinging to His promises and His peace, glorifying Him in the church and in Christ Jesus (Ephesians 3:21). May He move mountains with your mustard seed of faith as He has with mine.

Sincerely,

Dr. Alanna F. Bree

A Children's HOUSE For Pediatric Dermatology

A Children's HOUSE For The Soul

About A Children's House

"But Jesus called the children to him and said,
'Let the little children come to me, and do not hinder them,
for the kingdom of God belongs to such as these.'"

– LUKE 18:16

BEFORE I TELL YOU about A Children's House, let me tell you something you may not know about skin disease: It's more common than you might think. Skin disease affects approximately 20% of children and teens, and significant birthmarks affect about 5% of the population. But unlike other medical conditions, children with a skin disease do not have a choice about sharing it with others. They wear their disease every day; it is the first thing that others notice about them.

That's where we come in. A Children's House for Pediatric Dermatology provides exceptional pediatric dermatology care and an extraordinary patient experience that consistently exceeds expectations. We are blessed and privileged to welcome infants, children, adolescents, and teens to our charming neighborhood office located in Houston, Texas. We diagnose a multitude of simple and complex skin, hair, and nail conditions and perform a variety of treatments that are sensitive to the developmental stage of our patients. Our focus is on compassionate, holistic care that is reasonably priced with flexible appointments.

Fortunately, most skin conditions and associated symptoms—such as itching, discomfort, pain, or secondary infections—can be improved by a medical or surgical treatment. In severe cases, these treatments are anything but benign and may include the need for daily full-body dressing changes that can be painful and time consuming, as well as periodic use of intravenous infusions, daily or weekly injections, and chemotherapy agents to suppress the condition. Other conditions may require repeated laser therapies or surgeries that can be painful and that require time for recovery. Unfortunately, many skin conditions, especially genetic-based or inherited conditions and extensive birthmarks, still do not have any available treatments, and there are no known cures.

But even with treatment, skin disease is more than skin deep. In fact, one study compared the health-related quality of life for children with chronic skin conditions to other chronic diseases of childhood, including diabetes, epilepsy, asthma, kidney disease, and cystic fibrosis. Chronic skin disease was ranked second compared to cerebral palsy in regard to impairment of quality of life.

This leads to a profound effect on the psychosocial development of a child who is affected by skin disease. Two out of five children with a chronic skin conditions have some psychosocial impairment, including social withdrawal, lack of confidence, and depression. It has been found that the degree of impairment does not always correlate to severity of the condition, which is not surprising considering that some Americans spend more on their appearance than on health and education combined. Our society values external beauty and conformity with aesthetic standards, which unfortunately leads to social stigma, alienation, and bullying of individuals affected by skin disease and birthmarks. As a result, these affected children internalize the consistent negative reactions from others and often suffer from a lifetime of poor body image and low self-esteem. They feel all alone and isolated, and they often hold the belief that no one can understand what they are going through.

Parents of children with skin disease and birthmarks also face special challenges. Often, they feel guilt, shame, and helplessness. They see how others stare at their babies and children, and they are often asked rude and upsetting questions about the conditions affecting their children. In extreme cases, some families are even reported to child protective service agencies based on the misconception that they have precipitated the condition by abuse or willfully neglected it by withholding treatment.

This is where our nonprofit organization comes in. A Children's House for the Soul, which is fully sustained by A Children's House for Pediatric Dermatology, is dedicated to encouraging and uniting children and teens affected by skin disease and birthmarks, along with their families, by providing desperately-needed support on a regular basis for these underlying psychosocial and emotional issues. There is no other organization in the Houston area that provides similar services; therefore, it fills a unique need.

Thankfully, we have the opportunity to bring together individuals with similar struggles around facilitated activities and discussions, like at our "Love the Skin You Are In" events, that help them feel connected, validated, and understood. They realize they are not defined by nor limited by their skin disease, and they learn powerful coping strategies. Most importantly, it is my personal goal that each child who is touched by our organization knows without question that he or she is God's masterpiece, created anew in Christ Jesus, so they can do the good things He planned for them (Ephesians 2:10).

With this support, these children and teens begin to accept themselves as they are. This leads to positive awareness, empowerment, improved body image, and self-esteem. Their newfound coping strategies help them persevere through challenges, avoid social isolation, and positively address bullying. As empowered members of our community, they are strengthened and able to be advocates for

Our dedicated volunteers at our "Love the Skin You Are In" event

themselves and for others who suffer from similar issues, and they can pursue opportunities they may not have otherwise undertaken.

In sum, A Children's House is helping children and teens affected by skin disease and birthmarks to rewrite their stories with the potential for changed lives. I know this is possible because of the miracles that I have witnessed in my life and in this process, which make me all the more determined to share God's message of grace through forgiveness and hope in salvation through His one and only Son, Jesus Christ. Regardless of a person's profession of faith, my prayer is that every child, teen, or parent who enters A Children's House sees the love of Jesus here on Earth in the care that is provided.

A Children's House

I warmly invite you to find out more by visiting us at:

A Children's House
713-942-9357
www.achildrenshouse.com
www.achildrenshouse.org
1976 West Dallas Street
Houston, Texas 77019

About the Author

ALANNA F. BREE, M.D. is a board-certified pediatric dermatologist and owner of A Children's House for Pediatric Dermatology, where she specializes in effective treatments for skin disease and birthmarks, including pediatric dermatologic surgery. In addition to her private practice, she is currently serving as a Clinical Assistant Professor of Dermatology at Baylor College of Medicine and exercising privileges at Texas Children's Hospital and The Woman's Hospital of Texas. She has been awarded six grants and more than 27 recognitions for her work, including twice named "Houstonia Magazine Top Doctors," "Best Doctors in America Award," and Castle Connolly's "Top Doctors". She has also been recognized as a Bear of Distinction for Excellence in Public Affairs by her alma mater, Missouri State University.

A Children's House is Dr. Bree's second book. Her research has appeared in more than fifty-three publications, including as co-author of her first book, *The Illustrated Manual of Pediatric Dermatology* (2005). She has served on five review panels, including as editor of the *Practical Dermatology Journal*, Pediatric Dermatology Section (2004-2006). She has also taught more than 45 courses at institutions such as Baylor College of Medicine and Texas Children's Hospital and has presented more than 70 lectures for organizations around the nation, including pharmaceutical companies. Her many media appearances include *Inside Edition* and Fox News.

Dr. Bree has been an active member of eight professional societies, including previously co-chairing the Pediatric Dermatology Expert Working Group for the World Health Organization (WHO) International Classification of Disease (ICD) revision project. Currently, she serves as secretary of the Scientific Advisory Council for the National Foundation for Ectodermal Dysplasias (NFED).

In addition to her private practice, Dr. Bree is also the founder and executive director of a 501(c)(3) nonprofit organization called A Children's House for the Soul, which provides social, emotional, and spiritual support

About the Author

that encourages and unites children, teens, and families in the Houston area who are affected by skin conditions and birthmarks. Her personal mission has reached children around the world through several short-term mission trips to Nicaragua, Guatemala, Kenya, and particularly Tanzania, where she has a heart for orphans with albinism. She has also volunteered with more than twenty-two other national education or health organizations, including co-directing the American Academy of Dermatology's Camp Discovery Texas for children and teens with severe skin conditions.

Dr. Bree enjoys spending time with her friends and family, including her husband, Doug, and their two children, Sam and Kendyl. She is active in her church, Trinity Lutheran Downtown, as well as in several community organizations. She loves traveling, eating good food, and making other people happy. She also specializes in taking lemons and making lemonade!